T0221220

SHORT SIMS
A GAME CHANGER

BY CLARK ALDRICH

Short Sims:

A
Game
Changer

Clark ALDRICH

Create powerful,
interactive educational
content in days not
months

FOREWORD BY KARL KAPP, ED.D.

CRC Press
Taylor & Francis Group
Boca Raton London New York

CRC Press is an imprint of the
Taylor & Francis Group, an **informa** business

CRC Press
Taylor & Francis Group
6000 Broken Sound Parkway NW, Suite 300
Boca Raton, FL 33487-2742

© 2020 by Taylor & Francis Group, LLC
CRC Press is an imprint of Taylor & Francis Group, an Informa business

No claim to original U.S. Government works

Printed on acid-free paper

International Standard Book Number 13: 978-0-367-86066-0 (Hardback)
International Standard Book Number 13: 978-0-367-85742-4 (Paperback)

Visit the Taylor & Francis Web site at
http://www.taylorandfrancis.com

and the CRC Press Web site at
http://www.crcpress.com

Contents

Foreword

I first met Clark in the back of a cramped van returning from some convention center in some faraway place back to the boring and drab conference hotel. The only bright spot in that hot van was our discussion of the concepts of games and simulations. He had just written his first book, and it was making quite the impression of the field. He had truly added a new dimension to the concept of games and simulations for learning. His book was published in the age of page-turner e-learning courses, and he was advocating for something more, something better. He urged designers to create instruction that was more than just a simple "Click Next to Continue" exercise.

Fast forward a few years. Clark and I are sitting in a dark room as advisory board members listening to a representative from an intelligence agency describe some type of training they are preparing to design and deliver. He leans forward and asks a few seemingly simple but ultimately insightful questions of the presenter. The room goes quiet. The gathered folks aren't sure how to answer his basic question. It was so simple, yet, so profound. The question and subsequent conversation turn the group towards a more productive and meaningful outcome.

Today, Clark has done it again with his concept of the "Short Sim." While many people have discussed at length the difficulty, challenges, and number of hours required to create a branching simulation, he has carefully thought through the problem. As a result, he's created a solution that makes the room go quiet. He has turned the simulation conversation towards a more productive and meaningful outcome. He has a knack for both forward thinking and simplification of the complex. Both of these "powers" are illustrated in this work.

Not only does Clark define the concept and provide actual working examples (something rare in books on these subjects) but he digs deeper and provides design principles, instructions for creating your own Short Sims and tips for getting out of the "linear thinking" mindset.

If you are tasked with developing instruction where you want the learners to have "competence and conviction," then you need to read and digest what Clark is describing in this work. He provides just the right level of depth, analysis, and practical tips and techniques to help you along your journey of the creation of your own Short Sims. He has re-conceptualized the simulation and made it approachable, practical, and meaningful.

Read and understand the nuances of the Short Sim, but then, go create them. It's what Clark wants you to do. The purpose of this book is action. Use the knowledge, examples, and case studies to create Short Sims, it's in the best interest of you, the field and, ultimately, of the learner.

Karl Kapp, Ed.D.
Professor, Bloomsburg University, Author, Researcher in
the Field of Games, Game Thinking, and Gamification.
Bloomsburg, PA,
January, 2020

Preface

Consider this question:

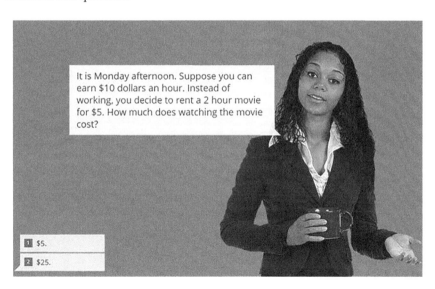

How would you answer?

In less than a minute, you have likely invented the theory of Econ 101's *opportunity cost*, without any instruction, exotic technology, or agita. We can add more graphics, narratives, and complexity, but this is a kernel of learning through Short Sims.

Author

Clark Aldrich is an education technology thought leader—the author of six books and developer of patent and award-winning projects. He currently builds custom Short Sims for organizations using a revolutionary methodology he has pioneered, or helps them build their own, through www.shortsims.com. He is also the host of an audio series called Education X Media (www.edbymedia.com) about evolving pedagogy in academics, corporations, and the military. He has been called a "guru" by *Fortune* magazine and a "maverick" by CNN. Aldrich and his work have been featured in hundreds of other sources, including CBS, ABC, *The New York Times*, *USA Today*, the Associated Press, *Wall Street Journal*, NPR, CNET, *Business 2.0*, *BusinessWeek*, and *U.S. News & World Report*. He has written monthly columns for *Training Magazine* and Online Learning Magazine. Previously, he was the founder and former director of research for Gartner's e-learning coverage. Earlier in his career, he worked on special projects for Xerox' executive team. He also served for many years as the Governor's representative on the education task force Joint Committee on Educational Technology, volunteered on several non-profit organizations aimed at child advocacy, and has served on numerous boards. He earned from Brown University a degree in cognitive science (during which he also taught at a leading environmental education foundation). He grew up in Concord, Massachusetts, and is the ninth great-grandson of Governors John Winthrop and Thomas Dudley, first and second governors of the Massachusetts Bay Colony, and Captain Walter Neale, the first colonial governor of lower New Hampshire.

The Short Sim

A Game Changer

The Necessity of Interactivity

Sid Meier, legendary creator of the Civilization series, said: "A game is a series of interesting choices."

This may be even more true of education.

There is a growing realization that significant interactivity in educational experiences is necessary for a successful learning program in more ways than we can count:

- Interactivity can allow the learner to *experiment*—and be creative, devious, or destructive—and see what happens.
- Interactivity can allow a learner to *customize their experience*, from engaging optional levels, to asking for more information only when needed, to choosing their preferred business or industry.
- Interactivity allows online *role-plays*, trying on different strategies and personalities.

- Interactivity allows the opportunity for participants to learn and deftly apply skills.
- And of course, interactivity can *test* a learner, to be sure—its current primary didactic use.

And because it gives learners control, even agency, interactivity can allow participants to develop *conviction*, a flexible and robust understanding of why a specific approach to a problem works, and often why their past behaviors or beliefs were not sufficient or successful.

Interactivity is more engaging than linear media and more time efficient. It helps learners to process and begin to own new information, not just cache it. Interactive media—including computer games—also engages new swaths of the target audiences, such as kinesthetic males, that have fallen through the cracks of most formal education programs.

On the other side of the coin, the act of *creating* interactive media changes the culture of the content producers. It shifts us from focusing on experts and top-down leadership to focusing on collaborating with the learners and considering their application of the knowledge.

From a pedagogical perspective, the more interactivity the better. Connecting user action with feedback has long been proven to be critical for most new neuron connections.[1]

The necessity of interactivity is why *educational simulations* and *serious games* have evolved quickly over the last couple of decades. They have grown from visionary experiments to predictable tools used to support the leading strategies of organizations as diverse as the U.S. Army and global corporations. The research tells us that interactive experiences work, and they can scale the development of *competency* and *conviction* better than other approaches.

Definitions

- *Simulations*: Functioning models of something else, designed for accuracy and predictiveness
- *Educational simulations*: Abstracted simulations with additional framing content, designed to develop skills or understanding in a user (e.g., flight simulators).
- *Serious games*: Educational material with additional framing content designed to make the learning fun and/or addictive, or games with educational elements (e.g., game shows or SimCity).
- *Gamification*: The use of framing content designed to make any activity more like a game and/or addictive.
- *Sims*: Interactive educational experiences that include both educational simulations and serious games.
- *Short Sims*: A sim distilled to its educational essence in content, design, and production.

---

[1] Held, R., & Hein, A. (1963). Movement produced stimulation in the development of visually guided behavior. *Journal of Comparative & Physiological Psychology, 56,* 872–876.

The Barriers

However, game-like interactivity is expensive to build. It is time-consuming. This content typically is platform dependent.

The inherent open-endlessness of games also makes them too challenging to work into assessment situations. Just sufficiently playtesting them is almost impossible.

And the skill set necessary to produce them is getting increasingly rarefied and expensive. This also means that existing educational games are seldom updated.

These conditions have prevented interactive content from becoming integral to educational media. Many organizations have been tempted, but have held off, or have built just one.

It is reasonable to assume that educational sims that follow the development path of today's computer games, even mobile apps, are not likely to currently grow beyond a niche until AI-augmented game programming becomes mainstream, which is at least eight years away.

The expectation of fully game-like experiences and lack of more focused examples has prevented highly creative individuals from being able to move ahead with interesting ideas. As a result, the most valuable part of sim design—re-imagining content with a "learning by doing" focus—has not been done in the scale needed and with the creativity needed.

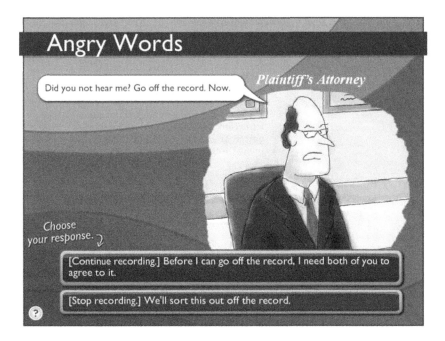

A role-play Short Sim using a *New Yorker* cartoon style

Until Now

That has now changed.

My question of the past few years has been, can we as instructional designers and educational media producers—enabled by this new technology infrastructure—find the synergy between meaningful interactivity and cost-effectiveness that is necessary for broad adoption? Can we meet the needs of both learners and sponsors?

To this, the answer is, after hundreds of pilots, yes. The answer is a well-tested development process that produces *Short Sims*. The new Short Sim methodology, presented here, can finally spark a new broad generation of authors and consumers.

Short Sims are a revolutionary new form of educational content, and the results have already been transformative. They fill in the single most important gap in educational media, learning by doing, in a way that is compatible with current academic and corporate environments, infrastructures, and skill sets. Short Sims can be created in the same time frame as linear content, such as traditional case studies, with the same work effort. They can also be edited, updated, and calibrated quickly. This means, for example, that a client can commission an online course, and the developer can add in Short Sims without significantly altering the delivery schedule or the budget.

Just as the combination of word processors and access to great examples has enabled authors (and video cameras and the work of past auteurs enabled directors), so too is a new generation of interactive creators now freed up.

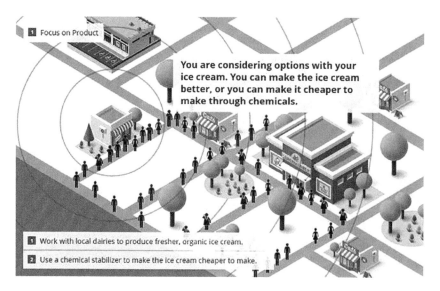

A Short Sim around the exploration of interesting system

Yes, But What Are Short Sims?

Short Sims are a new type of educational media—five to twelve minutes long—with few words and many decisions. They are streamlined online experiences made up of actions, goals, challenges, solutions, mistakes, and consequences. They tend to focus around a single subject area, and they can be embedded in traditional course material. They are intuitive to engage by design, typically with a multiple choice interface.

- **Short Sims:**
- Are a growing type of online educational content.
- Take between five and fifteen minutes to play.
- Are interactive.
- Are better at developing competence and conviction than traditional content.
- Share some attributes with computer games, including being replayable, visual, and responsive.
- Can be included in web pages or documents anywhere video or diagrams are.
- Are simple to use, typically with a multiple choice interface.
- Can be built from scratch using existing authoring tools in about two weeks.

Alone or alongside other educational material, Short Sims can achieve program goals from deeper understanding and conviction building, to understanding the application of processes, to user enjoyment and engagement.

The underlying approach of Short Sims may best be described as a simulation of a simulation—a complete set of static, non-linear storyboards that are connected together through links to create the sensation—and meet the pedagogical goals—of dynamic interactivity at a fraction of the time, cost, and requisite skill set. From a production perspective, a Short Sim is to a computer game what a comic book is to an animated movie.

They may be embedded in the longer document, such as in an HTML-based textbook, alongside paragraphs, charts, and short videos, and may be introduced in the material.

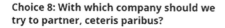 OK.

Choice 8: With which company should we try to partner, ceteris paribus?

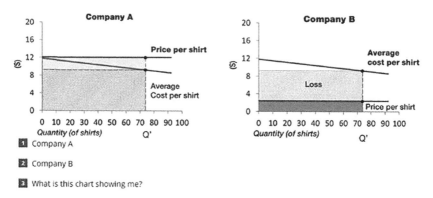

[1] Company A

[2] Company B

[3] What is this chart showing me?

A moment in a Short Sim around complex process

Typically, a course or chapter will involve multiple Short Sims. And due to their length, users may play some Short Sim three or four times, exploring different options. And Short Sims, unlike more complicated games, can also be fully handicap accessible.

⇨ Short Sim Authoring Tools

Short Sims can be made using a variety of both general and specialized tools. The list when this book was published includes

- BranchTrack
- iSpring
- Articulate <https://articulate.com/>
- Twine <http://twinery.org/>
- H5P <https://h5p.org/branching-scenario>

Quick Start Guide

For those who want to build their first Short Sims as fast as possible, look for the arrow icons (⇨), as follows:

- Find an authoring tool from the section above.
- Create a linear Short Sim, such as <www.shortsims.com/ch01>

- Reach Chapter 2, and play Be a Hacker.
- Create a simple branching Short Sim using the decision framework in Chapter 2.
- Optionally read Chapter 6 for Research.
- Follow the walk-through on Chapter 7, and create some smaller version.

"Low-Hanging" Learning Objectives

I have built Short Sims for organizations as diverse as The Bill and Melinda Gates Foundation, leading corporations, and large government agencies.

Some consistent low-hanging goals of Short Sims have emerged:

- Teach predictable processes
- Teach dynamic processes
- Present simple role-plays
- Present complex role-plays
- Inculcate a new ways of thinking
- Allow exploration of interesting systems
- Allows dynamic case studies
- Assessments.

Going Beyond Early Examples

While there are early patterns of uses forming, Short Sims are ultimately an open-ended approach. In my two roles—delivering finished Short Sims to clients and working with them to help them build their own—the only limit I have seen is the creativity of the designers. We have inherited the equivalent of a word processor. We have new topics that need interactivity, and learners who demand it. The only thing we no longer have is an excuse.

Short Sims have produced very high employee satisfaction scores and greater class completion rates in colleges compared to traditional media. The more students and instructors engage Short Sims, the more Short Sims become their expectation for educational content. We have already built and tracked textbooks that use Short Sims, and many students now look for the interactive segments and play them in a chapter before reading or watching anything else. And they learn well from them.

Numerous corporate training organizations have committed to shifting their own deliverables to greatly increase meaningful interactions for their learners through Short Sims.

The greater revolution will come when the next generation of authors, native to interactivity as *de rigueur* for education, will evolve all pedagogy away from *directive* and *passive* to *collaborative* and active. This changes everything and will finally render obsolete today's educational practices.

For Whom Is This Book and What Does It Cover?

This book introduces a new form of interactive content, called Short Sims, which will greatly help any organization that produces or uses educational media. Short Sims combine the time frames and flexibility of traditional linear content with the engagement and "learning by doing" nature of educational simulations.

This book is written for publishers, training organizations, professors, students, and government. It will combine the theory behind Short Sims with a process for development using—but agnostic of—some current development tools—illustrated with numerous illustrations including access to live examples.

Every breakthrough in education, from personalized learning to more accurate assessments to MOOCs to adaptive learning platforms, requires a better model of granular content. Short Sims finally do this.

2

Short Sim Example

Be a Hacker

Overview

A single play through of this Be a Hacker Short Sim takes just a minute or two. Quickly and efficiently, most learn a simple but interesting "aha" moment experimentally.

Try it for yourself by using this link to Be a Hacker: www.shortsims.com/ch02.

A Walk-through (Spoiler Alert)

In Appendix 4 is an optional walk-through that should be accessed only if the sim is not accessible.

Some Design Notes

This Short Sim took about ten hours to create, including interviewing the subject matter expert, who came up with the specific example in the situation during a broader interview.

A Single Story "Beat" Connects Beginning and End

This is a simple encounter, with only a single story beat. The *starting condition* (stolen password) quickly leads to a conclusion, with no shifts in tone or goal. But even with simplicity, the structure and language obscure the "right" answer enough to allow people (which we will call "player," "learner," or "student') to make a real-world rookie mistake.

The Core Mechanic

The sim uses a version of the same core mechanic of almost all Short Sims: a set up and decision moment, with choices between common mistakes and the right answer. This simple approach is nearly infinitely expandable. And, just as importantly, is easy and efficient to debug. There will be no unpredicted outcomes. ⇨ For fledgling designers learning how to use whatever authoring tool they have, start by creating any experience that uses this structure.

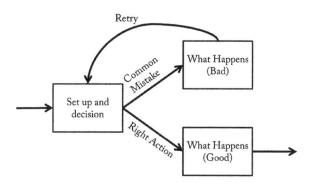

A core mechanic of Short Sims

Restrained Design

Technically, this hacker sim is made up of twenty-five screens (aka slides, aka panels), shorter than the average Short Sim of about eighty screens.

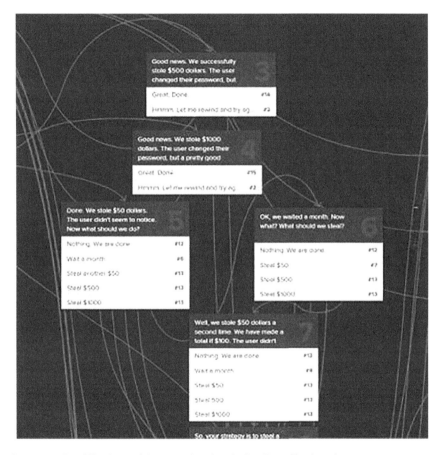

An example of the branching mechanism in the Be a Hacker sim

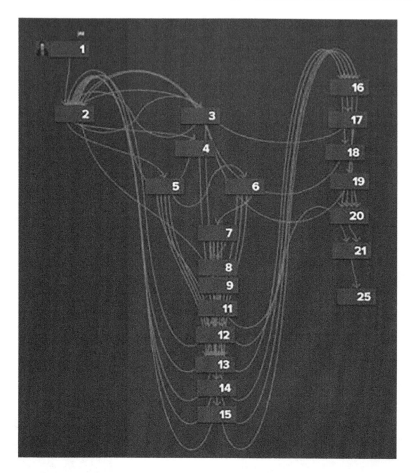

The entire Be a Hacker sim structure

It is also even more restrained in terms of development than most, with one generic character and one generic set. The character is made up of five static pictures that came with the sim authoring environment, that each conveys a different emotion: neutral, mild happiness, significant happiness, confusion, and disappointment. The set is just a photograph. There is no custom art. (Over time, New Yorker cartoon style graphics may prove to be more perfect, but are not readily available today.)

As with most Short Sims, the lack of expensive media, including audio and video, decreases creation time and, as importantly, increases the ability of the author to iteratively tweak the experience. This is akin to why authors write better in a word processing program than a page layout program. Anyone who found the hacker experience intuitive and frictionless can appreciate the role of minimum technology in making that happen.

Non-Directive Learning

This Short Sim is an example of non-directive learning. In traditional directive learning, information is pushed at a student, as is almost necessary in a book, video, or lecture. Directive leadership tends to get short term results, but often no, or even negative, long-term results.

Instead, here, the users have some freedom to make choices. It is closer to collaborative learning. Players are their own labs. The voice of the sim is not that of an evaluator. The on-screen character is designed to be a friend, helper, co-conspirator, and coach, not a person to be controlled or whose approval is all important.

This Short Sim follows an important design principle: enable, but never force, a player to make a mistake or do something immoral.

Replayability

The sim is also designed for players to replay it. It represents "downhill" work not "uphill" work. It is short, not stressful, easy to finish. But it is a bit harder to do perfectly. Virtually, all people will go through it three or four times, despite the option to skip right to the ending; every play through after the first is voluntary.

⇨ Play a Few More Short Sims

Before designing a Short Sim, creators should play at least four, and start looking at them analytically. Identify a favorite, and identify one to be a role model for an upcoming project. A second "first" sim to try is Audio File.

- Link to Audio File: www.shortsims.com/ch02

The Outlines of a New Design Philosophy

Short Sims should be effortless to access and use, with few directions needed. But to design them well takes a new approach—some of which we see here—that requires as much unlearning of the traditional educational design philosophies as application of the new.

3

Seven Short Sim Design Principles

Short Sims are technology independent.

They are not defined by any specific interactive media authoring tools (although the sims in this book were created using either BranchTrack or Articulate Storyline). Nor do they require any special hardware configuration. They should be accessible anywhere browser-based content can run.

Instead, Short Sims can be defined by their adherence to the following principles.

Build Competence and Conviction through Player Actions

The role of Short Sims is to develop competence and conviction. Competence is how to do something, and conviction is the deeply held belief that something is important. The means allowing players to make mistakes and helping them experience why they are mistakes. Short Sims should show, not tell. The learning model should be discovery based, with players proving to themselves ideas. Text should be short, with a much greater role being given to visuals and interactions.

Quick and Easy to Engage and Replayable

Short Sims should be easy to start playing, without a set of directions needed, or even a separate download. And they should be both short—five to ten minutes—and rewarding enough to play through four or five times, both to win and to simply explore.

Quick to Build, Easy to Update

In terms of production time frames, Short Sims match other educational content. Unlike traditional serious games, building a few Short Sims can be done in a corporate time frame, relatively quickly.

They can also be changed quickly, based on user feedback. And Short Sims are easy to come back to and make changes as the world evolves, not just abandoned when done and the design team dispersed.

For now, this means resisting expensive video and other art assets as much as possible, even giving up the pedagogically superior *New Yorker* cartoon style for photographs. This early stage may require a philosophy akin to Henry Ford's "You can have any color you want as long as it is black."

Rigorous Underlying Model

No matter how short, the only worthwhile sims are the result of a deep and profound knowledge of the subject matter. The creation of a short sim includes identifying the interactivity that could support a dynamic serious game, but then only presenting the most interesting paths through it. They are, in many ways, sims of sims.

Coexist with Other Educational Content

Short Sims should be able to stand alone as a self-contained piece of content engaged by a player. But they also can coexist seamlessly with other educational content, including text, illustrations, and video snippets.

Collaborative not Directive Leadership: Think Sim as Assistant

Directive leadership is giving people orders and expecting them to obey. Collaborative leadership is working together to solve a problem. As much as possible, the dominant onscreen character should be there to help and support the player, not judge, although the coach may report back bad news in some cases. One ideal voice for the sim is Iron Man's Jarvis/Friday. The player should be allowed to be creative, even rebellious.

Simple Mechanics and Open-Ended Creativity

The power of a word processor is not the technology anymore, but to give writers the ability to write what they want, using any genre they want, and publish it anywhere. The power of Short Sims is to leverage simple technology to allow people to imagine any interface, and present any experience, and then be able to put it where people need it.

Short Sims are Perfect for...

Short Sims can serve a variety of purposes. Ultimately, they could be as widespread as short videos across media. Some communities have already been early adopters.

Corporate Training Groups

Short Sims are perfect for

- New employee training, because they can be used at the moment of hire.
- Sales training, because they focus on interpersonal communication.
- Candidate pre-screening, because they can measure attitudes and skills, while presenting the job.
- Ethics and cybersecurity, because they focus on competing goals.
- Complex role plays that help high potentials with difficult situations.

Short Sims were designed to solve the unique problems of corporate training.

- They are faster to create than traditional content, while accomplishing more.
- They are interactive and engaging, while being very simple to use.
- They are easy to debug quickly and predictably.
- They focus on "learning to do" not just "learning to know."
- They respect the time of the learners, often requiring less than ten minutes.
- Their deployment can provide real-time insight into the tone of the culture.
- They can be highly visual.
- They do not require exotic skills nor special technology.

Traditional Media Producers

Any media producer needs to adopt Short Sims.

- They seamlessly integrate into existing work.
- They are seen as higher value than text, diagrams, and often video.

Training Content Producers

Groups that provide content for a living to corporations or other enterprises must adopt Short Sims as part (not all) of their deliverables.

- They are higher value.
- They are more aligned with the skills needs of large enterprises.
- They can be created quickly. They can be changed quickly, based on client feedback. They can be modified later, even if the original author has left.

Schools

Short Sims greatly increase the influence of instructors.

- They provide more self-study, while shifting the role of instructors from repetition to higher value coaching activities.
- They bridge the gap between lecture and exercises.
- They speak to younger generations.

Assessment

Short Sims were designed to support assessment. They are perfect for assessment for many reasons, including

- They provide a methodology for presenting multiple stage problems, including partial credit.
- They are 508 compliant.
- They are very simple to use, but still allow for a wide range of experiences.
- Short Sims produce a relatively small number of outcomes (perhaps five to ten), versus the nearly infinite outcomes of more dynamic models.
- They evolve from, and are compatible with, the item-creation culture of current assessment. An assessment company can transition current item-authors to Short Sims. The costs are aligned. They can coexist with traditional items on the same electronic page.
- There is no randomness, so they are always audit-able and fair.
- They allow for, but do not require, a transition into interpersonal dynamics, visual problem solving, short feedback loops, and next-generation skills such as leadership and adaptiveness.
- They reduce test fatigue.

Companies Seeking Cultural Influence

Any organization needing to drive change should adopt Short Sims.

- They are cost-effective.
- They are in demand. They can be dropped into the educational programs of others seamlessly.
- They are infinitely scalable.

- They build conviction and competence.
- Because they are often cloud based, they can be centrally changed.

Breaking with Academia's Dark Ages

Commonplace interactivity in educational media represents a bigger cultural revolution than most adults realize. It may change schools and universities so profoundly that we look back at these institutions "pre-interactive media" as being part of Academia's Dark Ages.

Given that, the process of creating Short Sims may rub some people the wrong way, especially if they are unconsciously biased towards traditional academic methodologies and outputs. It may be worth spending a bit more time onboarding colleagues on a development team who

- Prefer one answer and a single, linear path of success. They will argue against presenting gray areas as being "too complicated" or "too confusing" for the student to understand.
- Want to put instructions in a Short Sim before any decisions. They may personally hate making decisions where they do not know all of the information. Typically, older audiences fear making mistakes, but younger audiences would rather experiment first.
- Don't value the role of practice, and don't understand the pedagogy of presenting multiple scenarios that cover the same material from different perspectives.
- Believe all information should be presented. When faced with a Short Sim as a student, they want to go down every path and read every node. They may argue against different endings, or against having information be optional and only presented if the student asks for it.
- Want to consolidate screens. They would rather have one screen with three paragraphs than three screens each with one paragraph. (This is sometimes the right answer, but not always.) They think of user "clicks" as something to be minimized.
- Have a bias against using visual- and action-oriented metaphors. (See list at the end of Chapter 6.)
- Prefer directive over collaborative leadership. They believe the power is with the instructor/expert not the students.
- Prefer extrinsic rather than intrinsic feedback. To the player who made a mistake, they prefer to cite rules rather than show the natural consequences of making mistakes. (This topic is expanded upon in Chapter 12.)
- Don't personally enjoy interpersonal situations and lean away from using human interactions as a simulation interface.
- Are more empathetic towards the position of the lawyers and accountants and engineers than sales people or CEOs.

- Fight all humor and character in a sim.
- For the sim design, prefer completeness and accuracy over engagement and learning in an interaction. (They are bias against the philosophy that "a real F-16 cockpit is a terrible place to learn to fly.")
- Oppose easy, warm-up levels.

All his life, people had underestimated (and continue to misjudge) [Franklin Roosevelt's] native intelligence. The academic yardsticks at Groton, Harvard College, and Columbia Law had failed to measure his distinctive problem-solving capacity, to gauge his aptitude for seeing how disparate things connect, or credit the quickness with which he absorbed information. These unique aspects of his mind were often camouflaged by his outward geniality and easy charm of demeanor, leading members of his social circle to consider him a lightweight.

Doris Kearns Goodwin[1]

[1] Goodwin, Doris Kearns. *Leadership in Turbulent Times*. New York: Simon & Schuster, 2018.

4

Planning Assumptions and Expectations

For the people who plan projects, including those trying to create a response to a proposal, here are some guidelines that may help.

Estimating Time to Creation

It should take an organization the same work effort to create a replayable, seven-minute Short Sim (of roughly six levels) as it does to create a finished eight-page case study. I have been involved in both types of projects with groups that can do this level of work in a couple of weeks, but some cultures can finish it in a long weekend while others need six months to get final sign-off.

Here are three estimates for the time it takes to create projects of different lengths—measured in levels—using a light format tool, such as BranchTrack. The project has been broken up into four equal steps, with number of hours for each step. However, as always, your mileage will vary.

Creation Time Per Stage	1 Level Sim (in Hours)	6 Levels	12 Levels
Step 1: Research and concept	3	10	20
Step 2: Interface designs, structures, and broad art	3	10	20
Step 3: Decisions, logic, dialogue, and precise art	3	10	20
Step 4: Refining and review based on feedback	3	10	20
Total (in hours)	12	40	80

Note: Assume the Short Sim uses seven screens combined for the introduction and conclusion, and fourteen screens for each level. Assume each level has three significant decisions and optional definitions. These numbers are provided for high-level planning, but final Short Sims will vary significantly.

Time Sucks

One goal of most Short Sim design processes is speed. Some conditions can predictably *double* or *triple* the creation time frame:

- Authoring environments that use more extensive formatting.
- The number of decision-makers on the project goes from two to five.
- The target best practices to be developed are not known.
- Custom art is required, especially art that presents specific artifacts for interactions.
- Several versions for needed for different audiences. Every subsequent derivative product, even if very tightly aligned, takes about half as much time again.
- The topic is conceptual.

In situations where the settings and interactions are obvious, such as in a customer service situation, Step 1 can be cut in half. With multiple sims that have the same basic look and feel, Step 2 can also be cut in half.

Short Sim Roles and a Sample Designer Schedule for Outsourcers

Different skills are needed to create a Short Sim. An experienced designer can take on most of the roles and produce a finished sim by himself or herself. In a production environment, teams *may* involve (with percentages of effort per sim listed, in order of importance):

- *Designer*: The designer is given the topic area for the sim, and does the interviewing and other researching, high concept, art and interface design, structure and dialogue, and integration of comments from reviewers into the final product. (~75% of final product.)

- *Subject Matter Expert (SME)*: A subject matter expert understands the content. For most projects, the sim designer will need to interview the SME for about an hour. Projects that require the input of one or two specific people who are quite busy—as is the case with many corporate projects—may be delayed based on availability for initial research and subsequent review. Any project that requires an SME sign-off on the finished sim is doomed. (5% of finished project.)
- *Client Manager*: The client manager is the de facto lead of a sim project. They are the people who identify and secure the project to begin with. They then provide a constant voice of the customer throughout the development process. They may or may not be involved directly in the content creation process. They are constantly looking over everyone's shoulders and often making final judgment calls on tough decisions based on what they believe the client wants. The client manager may also assist the project manager and the lead designer in setting up a critical approval meetings, project pilots, and meetings with SMEs. (5% of final product.)
- *Project Manager*: The project manager has to be a master of precision and tact. They have to be there to support all of the other people and talents, and yet at the same time enforce deadlines and budgets through soft and hard power. The project manager also is responsible for the critical play testing of the sim. Ultimately, project managers have to be of high skill level and low ego. They report to the client manager. (15% of final product.)
- *Database Systems Integrator*: The database systems integrator is responsible for all integration of the program into the customer environment. This includes SCORM compliance, Learning Management System (LMS) integration, database integration, and knowledge of the end-user environments. This role often extends the furthest out, as client implementation environments change months or even years after the simulation has been successfully installed. On many implementations, this can take less than an hour per Short Sim, including testing. (2% of final product.)
- *Artist and Other Talents*: Projects may need custom art, custom voice overs, or other talent. However, each adds cost, adds time, and can reduce flexibility and long-term updatability. The ethos of Short Sims is to use clip art and other stock assets as much as possible, and no voice overs. (0%–5% of the finished product.)

Example of Ranges in Time Frames

With support, one experienced, internal, full-time sim designer can produce one sim a week.

A more conservative schedule of an external designer's part-time work for four medium-length, robust Short Sims with some supporting linear material, packaged as a finished, stand-alone course, is as follows:

Deliverable/ Milestone	Description of Deliverable/ Milestone	Actual Design Work (in Hours)	Due Date
Brainstorming conversation	Initial conversation to discuss goals and ideas.	1.5	Start day
Design plan	Plan describing the approach, instructional strategies, initial design concepts, and details for each module.	54	Start day + 3 weeks
Minimum viable product version (prototype)	Prototype version ready for initial end-user testing and internal review.	54	+ 5 weeks (start day + 8 weeks total)
Beta version (end-user pilot)	Beta version ready for pilot session with end users.	54	+ 7 weeks (start day + 15 weeks in total)
Gold version (final)	Final delivery that includes end-user feedback from pilot session.	18	+ 7 weeks (start day + 22 weeks)

Other Planning Best Practices

- When allocating designers, it is usually best not to assign less-experienced designer to multiple sims at one time. Sims require an immersion in the topic that is often diluted for newer designers when working on more than one topic.
- When planning milestones, it is best to target getting an imperfect prototype out as quickly as possible. This can then be calibrated based on feedback.
- Feedback sessions with SMEs and typical users are critical.

Sometimes, a Leap

Planning should be a bit fluid. The number of sim levels, even sims themselves, can evolve. A single sim may end up combining the contents that had been allocated for two. At other times, more content is needed to cover a single topic sufficiently. It is safer to say that Short Sim planning generally underestimates the number of levels required. And in more than a few projects on which I have worked, the topic proved big enough to warrant splitting single sims into multiple, shorter experiences. In some cases, creating a bigger sim takes less time than getting organizational consensus on which levels to take out for the sake of meeting the original scope parameters.

And the more conceptual or ambiguous a sim is (see the section "The Tolerance for Ambiguity" in Chapter 5), the more likely there will be some intellectual risks and some leaps of faith in the design. Conservative cultures may plan to build one extra Short Sim for every three.

5

Identify the Audience and Broad Topic Parameters

A Broader Audience

Sim designers have to understand their audience, including initial skill and interest level, language, and even technology platform.

However, the audiences for Short Sims can be defined significantly more broadly than for most educational media. This is because Short Sims, with their simple interfaces, establishment of situations, graduated-level design, satisfying feedback, and highly visual nature, are more accessible to larger swaths of the population. They are more technology agnostic—deployable in any browser environment, be it phone, tablet, or desktop (a standard screen minimum size does influence design). They self-adjust to people of different initial skill levels. And users even need a less comprehensive knowledge of the native language to learn.

The role of good design is to fully meet the needs of increasingly broader audiences. Yet there are still some decisions to be made.

Obviously, one wouldn't design a ship just to navigate in the average weather across the average depth of the ocean. One designs it for the edge cases. We must do the same for education.

The Tolerance for Ambiguity

Perhaps the single greatest audience-centric variable in creating Short Sims is setting their tolerance for ambiguity. Should a sim err on the side of play and exploration, or should the sim be lean and focused? Should a sim have labs and complicated interactions, or should the learner be spoon fed everything? Is the learning experience an immersive mini-sabbatical or an article to skim?

I like to think of three different levels of ambiguity for Short Sims.

1. The most direct Short Sim is efficient. It takes players through what is typically a linear process. It allows people to make mistakes, of course, but corrects them gently and immediately. The reasons to take the sim are self-evident. This approach focuses on competence. For a salesperson, the Short Sim would take them through a typical sales call.

2. The second kind of Short Sim may present some more interesting problems. These sims may use edge cases—unlikely but possible encounters—to come at the material from a different angle, in part to help players understand more fully the system dynamics of which they are part. This approach balances competence and conviction. For a salesperson, the sim Short Sim would take them through encounters with difficult or unusual customers.

3. The third kind of Short Sim is more like a lab or a game. It requires trial and error, and frustration, and resolution. Players experiment and learn from their mistakes. This approach develops conviction. For a salesperson, the Short Sim would put them in the position of their customer trying the run their business. In some cases, the Short Sim never explains itself explicitly and allows users to come up with their own theories.

Sims designed for the military or for business schools are typically in the third category, and reach an audience with a greater tolerance for ambiguity. They are happy to put in the time and thought, but they demand a rich and worthwhile experience. Salespeople, as a culture, demand easy-to-consume. A truism may be if a player sticks with it, the higher the frustration, the greater the learning.

Over time, however, the deployment of consistent high-quality educational media can shift a culture from wanting fast and easy to wanting efficient and meaningful.

Most tricky, any combination of sponsors and audiences typically does not present a unified front to this question. As a result, often the ambiguity-level drops one point from initial commitment to a sim and the final delivery.

Use beyond the Original Goal

As an unintended consequence of this wide-range appeal, Short Sims are typically used well beyond their original program. They are often shown to customers and almost inevitably used in related classrooms. They also, if my experience is a guide, have a very long shelf life.

Narrow the Topic

If identifying the audience can be done a bit more broadly, the necessity of narrowing the topic has to be done fairly tightly.

First, identify the topic for the sim. (For a longer list of types of *learning goals and program goals*, see Appendix 2.)

Initially, choose areas in a curricula where Short Sims are needed, such as:

- Where a firm foundation is required for subsequent learning
- Where, in the past, more traditional methods—including lectures, text, and videos—have failed to meet learning objectives (I like telling instructors to "give me the hard stuff. Give me the content that you dread teaching.").
- Where interactivity is needed to break up chunks of more linear content and engage the learner.

Then, define the learning objectives and determine how success of the program will be measured.

A six-minute Short Sim may replace about three text book or instruction pages, although cover the same material more meaningfully. At this point, answer the question, "how is this material relevant for the learner?"

Note: In one program, I was asked to add a Short Sim to every chapter in a textbook. In some cases, the Short Sim was to go near the front of the chapter to set a foundation, and in other cases, it was placed near the end of the chapter to pick up some advanced topic. To build the former type was easy, as they assumed little competence and conviction on the part of the student. But the sims that were end of the chapter had to build on usable knowledge that I had a hard assuming from the beginning of the chapter, and so those sims ended up being twice as long, with both foundation and advanced content.

Competence and Conviction

This "focus on focusing" should never detract from the real focus of the media. Ultimately, the raison d'être to do any sim is to drive *competence* and *conviction*. Sims do this better than any other media.

Competence is the ability of a learner to apply the right skills. It can even include use the right words. But developing conviction in an audience is even more important for most applications.

Conviction is the enduring understanding and drive in the learner to do the right thing. I look at the conviction level by gauging:

- How do people actually behave when no one is watching, and/or when stressed?
- Can people improvise the philosophies to appropriately adapt it to situations not covered in the formal course?

The combination of competence and conviction creates comfort. This is the ease that traditionally has come with real experience, especially experimentation. Comfort can be around using a new online tool, selling a new product or service in a new way and in a new environment, or leadership or project management. The ability of sims to create comfort is unique and valuable. Once an organization begins developing simulations, they understand why there old ways failed.

- We will dive more into how to do this throughout this book, but Chapters 13 and 14 are more helpful than most.

6

Research, Including Subject Matter Expert Interviews

No matter how short, the only worthwhile sims are the result of a deep and profound knowledge of the subject matter.

In some cases, this knowledge exists in the wild, such as in various online venues. In other more specialized cases, only a few people in the world may have the necessary insight. (And it is the opportunity to talk to such people that is part of the joy of being a sim designer.)

Do Outside Research

Research the material as thoroughly as possible, using as many outside sources as is feasible. Find the external world-class thought leaders where they exist. Use Khan Academy and TedX videos. Many have found that hearing experts *speak* is more valuable than reading what the same experts have *written*, because it is less edited.

Note: Even when client corporations or universities believe they have sufficient internal expertise for a sim, outside sources are invaluable. They provide a fresh perspective and in some cases surface issues or problems that internal experts would never consider.

Interview the Subject Matter Experts

For most sims—such as around computer programming, negotiating, or living a satisfying life—there are just two central questions for subject matter experts (SMEs):

- What are the right ways of doing this?
- What are common mistakes in this area?

Then, organic expansions of this core question can sufficiently result in great Short Sims. Follow up questions include:

- What happens when wrong decisions are made?
- Why do people make mistakes?
- What are tricky situations that may confuse newbies or experienced practitioners? Which situations would result in participants asking questions of colleagues, and which are mistakes people make without realizing they are making mistakes?
- What are different outcomes in this area, good and bad?

These questions assume an action-oriented, "learning to do" perspective. Where there is not an obvious protagonist doing the doing, such as an academic sim about water cycles or a business sim about process integration, sometimes a few different first person perspectives have to be explored.

Note: One difference between a sim interview and other types of interviews is the amount of specifics you will need. For example, consider an interview moment, when the expert you are interviewing explains that when a legal client calls you with a question to which you do not know the answer, the right answer is to look up the official wording in some online resource. My follow-up questions are along the lines, "Do you admit to the client you do not know the answer? What words would you use? Do you put the client on hold? Do you call them back with the answer? Do you email it? Do you talk to them while you find the right answer?" And after each question, I might ask both "Why" and "What would happen if you did it some other way?"

Note: I always record conversations with experts, with their permission. I end up listening to these four or five times, and pick up different thoughts each time. The very specific phrases used by the experts provides the volume of precise verbiage that any sim requires.

Some researchers prefer to send ahead or otherwise be equipped with a longer, richer list, especially for more complicated subjects. See Appendix 3.

Note: Never give internal SMEs control of the process or final say on the content (unless they are the direct client or the author). Some will tinker and tinker until all of the budget is gone. And in situations when necessary expertise is concentrated in a few people who are not part of the core development team, the time to complete the Short Sim will increase by about 20%, both because of initial scheduling and subsequent reviewing.

A one-hour SME call can produce the raw material for one 7–10-minute sim. It takes me up to five hours to review each hour of recordings. When tackling a conceptual sim, I take notes in a word processor with the next goal of producing a design document. But in production mode for more linear processes, I type each note as a node directly in the sim authoring environment (see the next chapter for specifics).

On Experts' Use of Visual Metaphors

Some very smart, typically academically trained people use a lot of big and conceptually precise words and phrases to describe a situation (such as "Orthogonal" and "Force multiplier"). Others may introduce classic metaphors (such as "Manifest Destiny" and "The Sword of Damocles"), based on cultural literacy. At best, this manner of speech is highly illuminating within a given in-group, and at worse, it is a form of intellectual vulgarity, the artifact of cultures that prioritize impressing over communicating.

The best SMEs for creating more ambitious Short Sims speak in highly vivid, simple visual metaphors. They use basic examples or abstractions to make complex processes very clear. This is more typical of both military personnel and business leaders, and is an approach unfairly looked down upon by academics.

Perhaps the best example is the title of Lieutenant Colonel John A. Nagl influential book, *Learning to Eat Soup with a Knife: Counterinsurgency Lessons from Malaya and Vietnam.*[1]

Some other examples include

- I started poking the bear…
- …Too much fog of war…
- That was the secret sauce…
- That dog won't hunt
- That rubbed people the wrong way
- She was putting her thumb on the scale
- Roll with the punch…
- …Looking to scratch that itch
- Two steps forward, one step back
- Crash and burn

---

[1] Nagl, John A. *Learning to Eat Soup with a Knife: Counterinsurgency Lessons from Malaya and Vietnam.* University of Chicago Press, 2009.

- That idea ricocheted around the room…
- It went through the process like a pig through a python…
- Go outside and pound sand…
- There are three kinds of people: racehorses, Clydesdale, and donkeys….

(And, of course, the many sports analogies.)

Note: When I hear people talking in subtle academic terms around concepts, I think upper management. When I hear people talking in bold visual metaphors around actions, I think CEO.

7

Blocking Out a Simple Short Sim ⇨

One of the most straightforward types of Short Sims teaches users how to follow predictable processes. The sims typically take learners through the target process, step by step. At the end of the sim, the player has a much better feeling for how the process will play out in the real world. Along the way, the player has the chance to make right and wrong decisions. A situation is appropriate for this most linear of Short Sims if there is, despite some different circumstances, basically one "right answer" to a situation.

When the Short Sim covers such well-understood, linear process—such as completing a preflight checklist, solving math problems, or helping a customer at a service desk—the process, from interview notes to finished sim, is similarly predictable.

These sims have a single end-to-end path, with fewer endings (or just one), and less room for player personalization or improvisation. This is one reason why, while many Short Sims are designed to be replayed three or four times, these are not.

These steps are also foundational, but insufficient, for more complicated sims.

More Complicated Short Sims

This approach, for mapping out linear, well-understood processes, changes significantly as sims tackle more strategic issues. Some of the possible differences in initial designing, in the order they must be resolved, include

- *Unknown best practices*: In some cases, an organization may not know the best practices, or even learning objectives, of a program. Research can take weeks or months.
- *Unknown interactions*: Often, what the player will do in a sim is unknown. For example, in an academic sim about water tables, the system itself may be well understood, but there is little intrinsic guidance to the sim designer on who is doin' the doin'.
- *Unknown scenarios or settings*: Often, the roles and the objectives are known (i.e., salespeople need to be able to sell cloud services to customers of installed software), but the exact situation to be modeled is less clear.
- *Unknown types of levels*: Some sims require different types of levels to develop the necessary competence and conviction. A sims may switch between discussion and labs, or between action and theory.
- *Unknown logic*: The logic for the simple processes above may be incredibly basic, but more interesting sims will use more interesting logic. For example, one sim approach will be to, instead of having just one central sequence, have branches that take the narrative in different directions, or to have a more open-ended labs, such as in the last level of the Demand Curve Sim in Chapter 13. As a rule, however, the more complicated the logic, the longer the sim will require to test, and the higher motivation the player will need to productively engage the sim.

A Review of Basic Sim Authoring

Here is a short video with some of the basics of sim authoring, using BranchTrack and the Be a Hacker sim: www.shortsims.com/ch07

Before following this full process, first time authors should create a few Short Sims, just to get the hang of the interface. This could include a conversation with a single yes/no branch, or even a simple linear progression.

- A Simple Short Sim: www.shortsims.com/ch07

First, Create Notes

I listen to the audio recordings of expert interviews and take notes, sometimes using tools like "oTranscribe". I tend to work directly in a Short Sim authoring to save time.

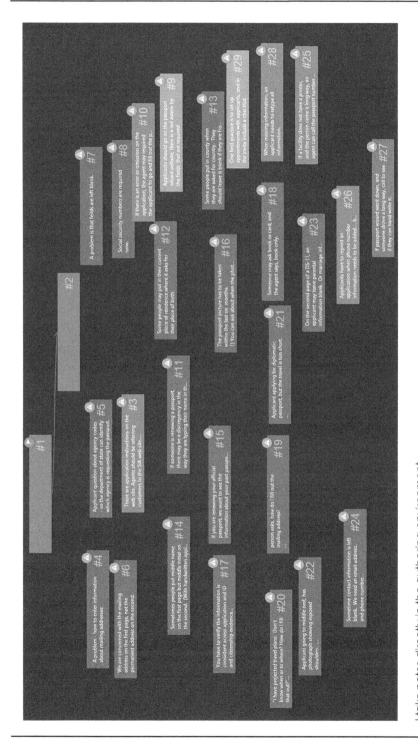

I take notes directly in the authoring environment

In the interview around a straightforward process, I look for the following categories, which I can color code:

- *Problems, Questions, and Rules that Must be Followed (Shown in #4–#8, #13–#24)*: These are places with right or wrong decisions. This can also include common questions that people have.
- *Fixes (Shown in #3, #10, #25, #26, #28)*: The best ways to solve problems. These can be associated with (put underneath) specific problems.
- *Best Practices (Shown in #9, #29)*: Ideas for minimizing the problems in the first place, or how to otherwise go above and beyond.
- How to Handle Unusual Circumstances (Shown in #27): Strange situations and how to handle them.
- *Background Notes (Also Shown in #9, #29)*: Small tidbits of information that may fit in as asides by the coach.
- *The Correct Sequence (#1, #2)*: The right steps in the process.

Storyboarding

The notes can then be organized and combined.

Horizontally, arrange notes that pertain to earlier steps in a process on the left of the screen, and notes that pertain to later steps in the process on the right.

Levels

Now, vertically, think about levels. Begin stacking notes into short, self-contained sequences. What are the moments and problems and decisions that can be used together? What might be some necessary setups? What are different kinds of interactions, from role play to lab to straight questions and answers that can be used?

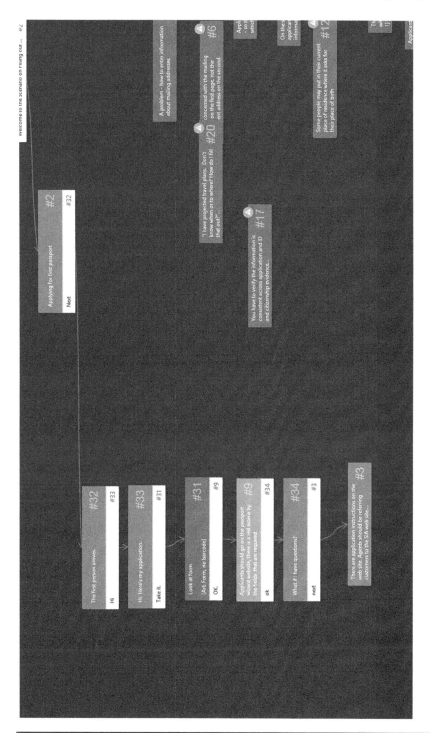

Organize Notes, and Optionally Add Set Up Nodes to More Closely Resemble the Final Sim

By the end of this process, most notes will be organized rigorously. Each level is represented by a single column, with the notes at the top representing the start of the level and going sequentially down. Each level should have both a starting point and places where decisions have to happen. When sims have multiple levels, as is almost always the case, the level columns will be organized from early levels on the left of the screen to later levels on the right.

In this case, a passport acceptance scenario, I decided that the entire sim takes place across one afternoon shift, and each level focuses on one customer. This sim is focused on how to find problems in a passport application, so the levels are organized, from issues or mistakes made at the *front* of the form to issues at the *end* of the form. Levels may further be combined or reordered throughout the process.

Calibrating the Flow

At this point, it is important for the designer to be able to "click through" the entire sim. We look to see if the high level flow works. We may reorder levels, realize we are missing content, or tighten redundant content.

As you go through, begin adding rough language, first draft characters, scaffolding nodes, and art placeholders. Some slides will just have narration. If you are planning on using a coach, now is the time to add that as well.

Don't quite yet begin building out the interactions around decisions. And just as sailor is reminded to keep the lines organized, so to play attention to how everything is organized. It will make editing so much easier going forward.

If helpful, create a temporary menu at the beginning of the sim to provide you with direct access to each level, using brief descriptors. This will not be part of the final sim, but it can save you time when editing.

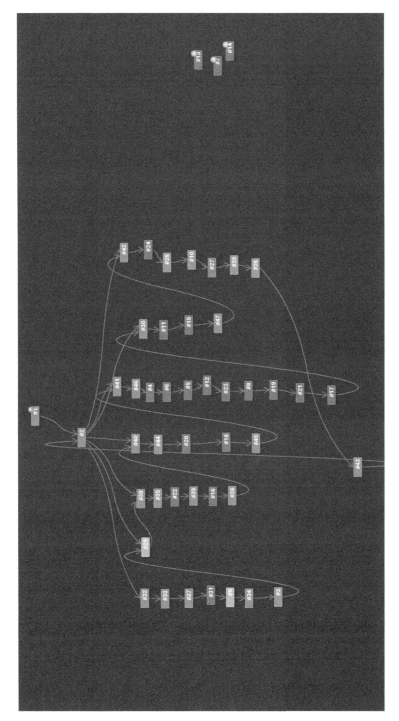

Start to organize notes into self-contained levels, with earlier steps on the left and later steps on the right. A few notes didn't make it to the sim (far right).

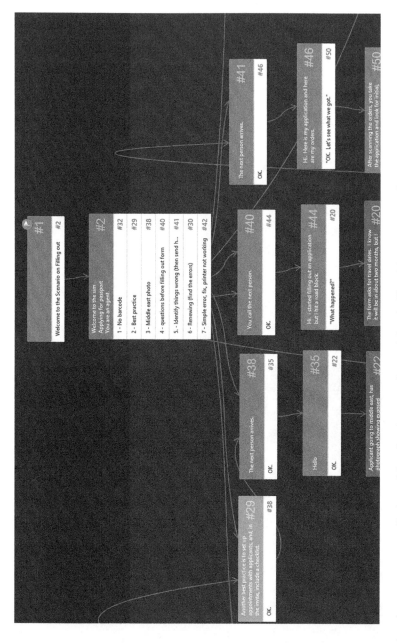

Create a temporary menu that provides direct access to each level with minimum description

7. Blocking Out a Simple Short Sim

Here is an example of how a note card of a problem may look at this point in the process as you step through it, as part of a level in the working draft version, but before the art, final character, and logic are added. This one slide could end up being between three and ten slides by the end of the process, depending on the approach you use.

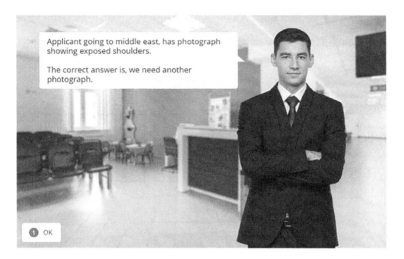

This note card for an interaction shows a neutral character, but will need cleaning up, a final character, art and logic.

Continue to go through the sim, adding and fleshing out dialogue with characters. It is disorienting to go through these broken clusters. Through iterations of editing, however, the flow gets smoother, the places where options make sense become more obvious, and working on the Short Sim is less taxing and more enjoyable. Levels may have to be slightly reordered, which can simply be done by changing the links, not necessarily moving the level columns.

Definitions

- *Sequence*: A sequence is what may happen in a sim, from beginning to end. This could be how to make a cake or how an important meeting unfolds. All sims have at least one primary "correct" sequence. Most sims also have many different overlapping sequences of various lengths, more of which will end in failure than success. (Sequences may also be called *paths* or *flows*.)
- *Setups*: Setups are the situations you create for the player to engage. What role is the player taking on, and what are the goals? The set up for some sims are easy and obvious, and for others quite hard. Setups are used for the entire sim, and often, more succinctly, for each level.
- *Decisions*: Decisions deal with choices the player will have to make. Some decisions are big, such as deciding to take a job, or flip a big switch that says, "do not touch." Some decisions are small, such as raising the price by ten cents or putting your left foot in, or insignificant. Decisions will all be reflected in the interface.

Refine and Add Interactivity

At this point, we will add the interactivity around the problems. We will also continue to go through the sim, doing the equivalent of sanding and caulking. We will add slides where necessary, finalize the characters, refine the dialogue, and start creating the missing art.

The easiest challenge to model is a simple right or wrong answer. I create those first.

Note: A generic, complete decision and immediate feedback screen sequence is

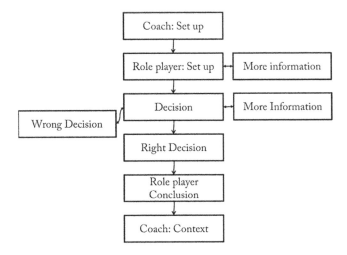

In our example, the sequence involves two learning objectives, shown as problems in #22 and #16:

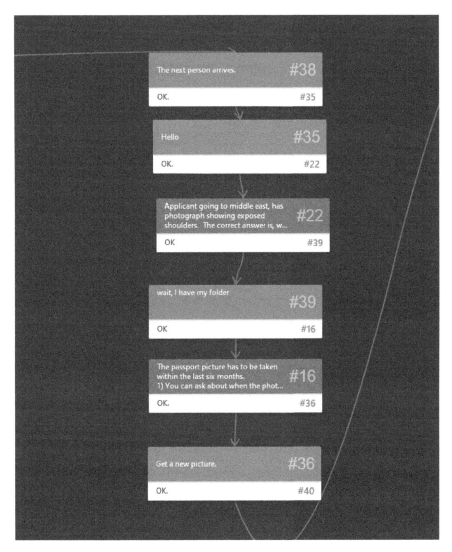

Take a piece of story board...

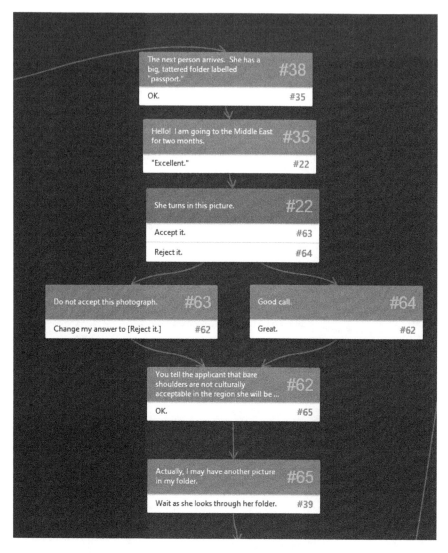

The next person arrives. She has a big, tattered folder labelled "passport." #38

OK. #35

Hello! I am going to the Middle East for two months. #35

"Excellent." #22

She turns in this picture. #22

Accept it. #63

Reject it. #64

Do not accept this photograph. #63

Change my answer to [Reject it.] #62

Good call. #64

Great. #62

You tell the applicant that bare shoulders are not culturally acceptable in the region she will be ... #62

OK. #65

Actually, I may have another picture in my folder. #65

Wait as she looks through her folder. #39

....And add interactivity and details. In this case, we are adding a simple, binary decision.

We filled out this segment to add two very simple choices.

I use a predictable format for laying out my sims. Every level and every decision are organized in a consistent way. This makes debugging easy, as there is seldom any problems in the logic, and when there is, you can usually just eyeball the architecture to find out almost instantly what it is.

The sequence plays out as such.

The applicant gives a detail.

Next, our coach—much as an acting teacher would in a scene study class—steps in and narrates. I also created this piece of custom art for the passport photograph, based on a stock character, using two free programs, Paint.net and Google's Picasa. However, at this point in the process, putting in an art placeholders often makes more sense. The player is given a simple binary decision of accepting the photograph or not.

The player gets a bit of feedback (slide #63 or #64, shown in the logic flow above) and then the reason why (#62, shown below).

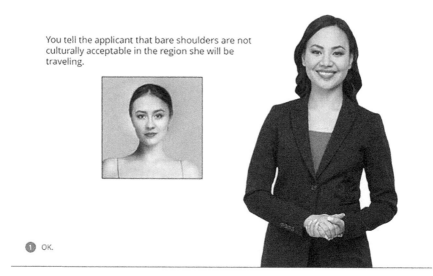

We then go to our second learning objective, keeping the same character, with the same setup and sequence flow we established in the storyboard.

We once again offer a binary choice.

And we again play a custom reaction (#66 or #67), and then a common explanation.

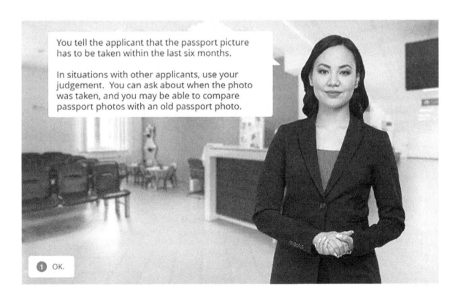

The above logic is incredibly simple. We can also make answers a bit more involved by using a minilab.

Another issue that the subject matter experts identified was that government employees may fill out passport applications in some way other than the online wizard, which produces a document that does not have the 2D barcode in the upper right hand corner. These applications are not acceptable.

So, we simulate the player, as agent, welcoming the next person in line, and being handed the passport form.

You begin to look at the form:

We first ask the player if they are going to accept the document (cell #37 below).

Adding Logic Around One Identified Problem

If the player does accept the passport application (cell #53), we tell him that there was a mistake, and immediately put the player back on the right track of identifying the problem.

Starting with cell #54, we cycle a gray circle around four different parts of the application, inviting the player to show what specifically is wrong.

Using this technique, experienced players who know the answer will go through the interaction quickly, while those that do not can figure it out, even if just by trial and error. This technique avoids one multiple choice problem of having to over-articulate the possible answers. (And, again, I often put in art placeholder at this point, but here are the finished screens that were assembled in PowerPoint.)

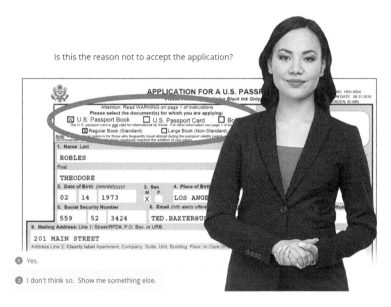

If the player chooses [Yes] incorrectly, such as above (#55), we present a bit of information and then return the main sequence.

Is this the reason not to accept the application?

APPLICATION FOR A U.S. PASSPORT
Please Print Legibly Using Black Ink Only

OMB CONTROL NO. 1405-0004
OMB EXPIRATION DATE: 08-31-2019
ESTIMATED BURDEN: 85 MIN

Attention: Read WARNING on page 1 of instructions
Please select the document(s) for which you are applying:

☒ U.S. Passport Book ☐ U.S. Passport Card ☐ Both
The U.S. passport card is not valid for international air travel. For more information see page 1 of instructions.

☒ Regular Book (Standard) ☐ Large Book (Non-Standard)
Note: The large book option is for those who frequently travel abroad during the passport validity period, and is recommended for applicants who have previously required the addition of visa pages.

1. Name Last
ROBLES

☐ D ☐ o ☐ Dep DOTS
End. # _____ Exp. _____

First
THEODORE

Middle
S

2. Date of Birth (mm/dd/yyyy)
02 14 1973

3. Sex
M F
X

4. Place of Birth (City & State if in the U.S., or City & Country as it is presently known.)
LOS ANGELES, CA

5. Social Security Number
559 52 3424

6. Email
TED.BAXTER@US.ARMY.MIL

7. Primary Contact Phone Number
225-555-0196

8. Mailing Address: Line 1: Street/RFD#, P.O. Box, or URB.
201 MAIN STREET

Address Line 2: Clearly label Apartment, Company, Suite, Unit, Building, Floor, In Care Of or Attention if applicable. (e.g., In Care Of - Jane Doe, Apt # 100)

① Yes.

② I don't think so. Show me something else.

Now, we show the right problem, which the player chooses. (If the player did not choose the right answer, he or she would go to one more wrong option (#60), and then cycle back to the first option (#54).)

1 OK.

You and your housemate will go together for errands. Your housemate is local and drives more efficiently. Who should drive?

	Get to		
You	4 Stores	in	2 Hours
Housemate	5 Stores	in	2 Hours

1 My housemate will drive. I will be the passenger.

2 I will drive. My housemate will be the passenger.

We then provide a bit of explanation.

Perfect. There is no 2D barcode.

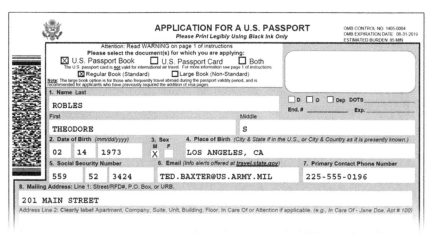

1 [Continue.]

And then show how it should look:

Passports that were created on the passport application wizard have barcodes, that contains all of the information from the passport.

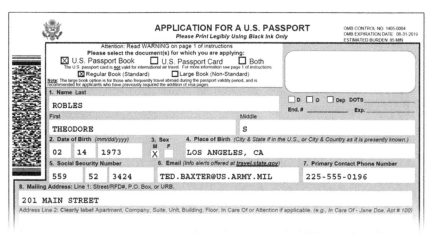

1 [Next.]

We use the coach to provide the right verbiage. This approach can minimize too much text in the player's options.

We have one more identified issue, the need for applicants to use the online resources. We could simply present that information, but instead I added a simple question.

The customer asks, "Do you have a phone number I could call if I have questions?" (#34)

I take a shortcut here, which is to create an interaction that responds with the right answer to either a right or wrong decision by the player.

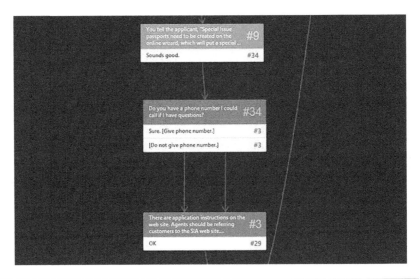

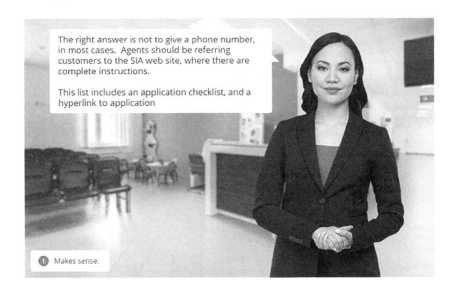

We then transition to the next person in line, which is level 2.

One piece of custom art had to be designed: the initial application that was missing the bar code. Then, five more variations were created: four screens with a highlight circle in four different places and then one final application showing what the right bar code looks like. I try to minimize the use of custom art, but of course use it whenever it helps. Whenever possible, I use PowerPoint to create the art and export it as a JPEG. Again, this greatly increases the ability for future authors to make small (or large) updates or corrections when (not if) problems are found.

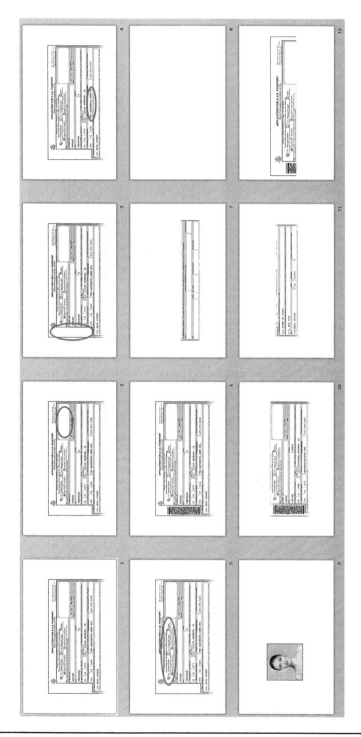

PowerPoint allows for quick changes and easy builds.

(At Some Point) Create an Introduction

At some point, we create the formal introduction and finalize both the introduction (taking out the temporary links to all of the later levels).

For our example:

Wrap Up

We can continue to expand the storyboard. A consistent, visual organization can make spotting problems and making small changes second nature. I also keep a temporary link on the first page which I label "Current." This takes me to the most recently finished level, which sets me up to tackle the next, unfinished level.

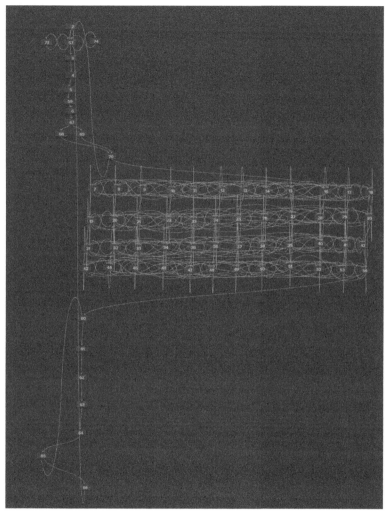

Almost Done Chart

Then, as was done with all of the sims in this book, we finish the conclusion to the sim always giving the player the opportunity to restart. This is very helpful for us as designers, as well as not a bad expectation to make all sims more accessible.

8

Getting Feedback

One of the most important parts of the Short Sim development process is getting feedback before the launch. This often is solicited from a variety of camps:

- Initial Design
  - Feedback from colleagues
  - Feedback from subject matter experts (SMEs)
  - Feedback from project sponsors
  - Sign offs from gatekeepers, such as lawyers.
- Pilot
  - Feedback from typical end users
  - Feedback from project sponsors.

And one appeal of Short Sims is their relative ease, at least compared to other interactive content, both for testers to *give* useful comments and then for the designers to *make changes* based on these comments.

Having said that, getting feedback for Short Sims, even using current best practices, still feels a bit ungainly. The compensation for this, however, is we do see immediately how much better our sims are with every new perspective.

Feedback during the Initial Design

Throughout the creation process, a Short Sim designer takes sharps swerves, from the *introversion* of fact finding, to the *extroversion* of interviewing experts, back to the *introversion* of design, and then back to the *extroversion* of getting feedback. For most people, half of this work will be downhill and the other half uphill. The right tools and processes make both types of activities easier.

Set Up Temporary Links

In some cases, when showing a Short Sim to reviewers, it is useful to have some special "review-only" links. Two places:

- In the first or second slide of a sim, put temporary "review-only" links to each of the levels.
- After every big decision, put a "review-only" link after each conclusion, so the reviewer can go back and check the other options.

The Best Tool: In-Sim Commenting Tools

Many of the better short sim authoring environments provide dedicated reviewing environments. Here, reviewers are invited in and play the sim with the ability to make comments on any current slide. This is incredibly convenient for both the reviewers and the designers, but reviewers may walk away feeling that they did not see absolutely everything.

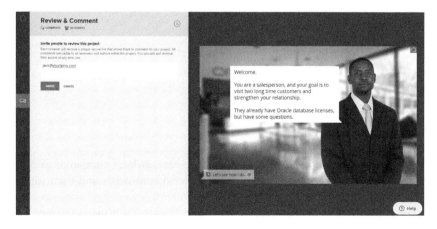

Sim designers using BranchTrack can invite in reviewers.

Reviewers get an invitation.

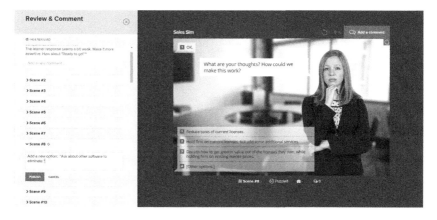

Reviews get a special ability to add comments per slide.

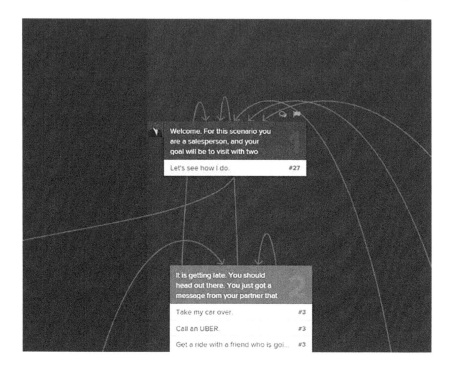

The designer sees any unresolved comments.

A Marked Up Word Document

A useful repository for feedback during the most of the Short Sim development process is a Microsoft Word document (or Google Docs). There are two different versions of this approach.

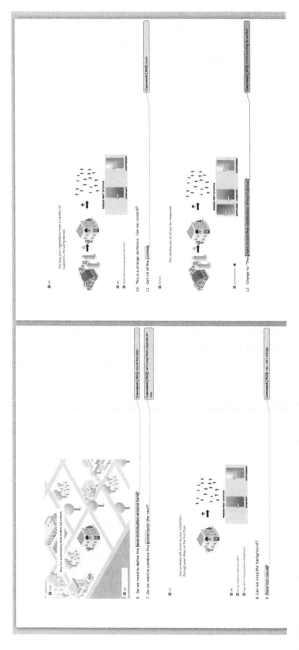

A Word Document can serve as a comment repository.

In one version, reviewers go through the sim, and when they find problems, copy a screenshot, paste it into the document, and then write their correction. Typically, the screenshots and concomitant corrections are presented in the order they appear (or encountered by the reviewer).

If the document is shared, subsequent reviewers may both add new screen shots and changes, or they may comment (hopefully in markup mode) on past comments.

In a second version of using Word documents, especially when seeking comments from lawyers, the designer presents complete scripts for marking up. This second version is almost always time-consuming to assemble, but results in a faster time to completion when gatekeepers have to be involved.

Directions for Commenters

Regardless of the method, ask commenters to provide, if possible, verbatim replacements for the text they want changed, or in other ways are as absolutely specific as possible.

Play through with the Clients

Another approach is to, often over a video tool such as WebEx or GoToMeeting, play the sim in front of the client and solicit their comments. The session can be recorded, and any changes can be made later while reviewing the comments. This is useful for a designer who wants to control the process, but the process can still be awkward to facilitate, with the combination of showing people, asking for any input, backtracking through decisions, and moving on without getting too convoluted.

During the Pilot Stage

Feedback is critical, and adequate resources—time and money—should be spent during the pilot stage of the process.

For Playtesters during the Pilot Stage

Once a Short Sim is ready, it needs to be put in front of sample end users (aka students aka users aka players aka learners). A project lead does not have to wait for the entire curricula to be done and can just playtest individual sections. Playtesting involves finding representative example of typical players and asking them to go through the experience. The best facilitators of the playtesting sessions say nothing, but just watch where the test users are confused. Obviously, the sim designers should not be anywhere near the sessions, but just shown the conclusions later.

Next, when the sim can be put in context, such as with the rest of a course, it can be presented to early audiences. Feedback can then be gained through surveys or interviews.

For SMEs and Sponsors of Complex Sims during the Pilot Stage

There is always a sign-off of the sponsors, and sometimes of the SMEs, before any release.

Feedback after Launch

At some point, the Short Sim is "done." (Leonardo da Vinci reportedly said, "Art is never finished, only abandoned.") But even if a sim is to support a short-term strategic initiative, they should remain change-ready.

Some thoughts:

1. All Short Sims are easy to change and update by design, even by authors who were not involved in the initial construction.
2. After Short Sims are launched, tracking metrics can be used to help determine where learning and engagement need to be improved (see "Measuring Learning and Learner Engagement" in Chapter 21).
3. When sims are cloud-delivered, they can be changed in real time. Everything from little errors to logic flows can be updated immediately.
4. Sims should be calibrated a week after launch, a month after launch, and a year after launch. In some cases, the "year after launch" activity may be to make a forked copy for use in a different venue. For example, a course designed to support a corporate roll-out may be forked for new employee training.

Embracing Mistakes

The most important thing a culture can do, at all levels, is to embrace mistakes. The more powerful the Short Sim will eventually become—the more it will challenge assumptions and represent new perspectives and best practices—the more mistakes will be made in the design process.

9

Types of Short Sims

Designers need to determine the general type of the Short Sim, influenced by learning objectives. All Short Sims bestow upon the users some experience; that is their birthright. The types in the next few chapters are optimized around Short Sims from simple to complex.

Inculcate a New Way of Thinking

In just a minute or two, a Short Sim can get users comfortable with a new way of presenting information or even a new way of thinking about a problem (Chapter 11).

Teach Predictable Processes

A straightforward type of Short Sims teaches users how to follow predictable processes, such as a bank teller cashing a check or making a deposit, a programmer writing a bit of code, a student solving an equation, or a pilot conducting a preflight checklist. These greatly speed time to comfort. These sims guide the user through the various steps of the process, and typically present two or three challenges per step (Chapter 7).

Present Labs

Short Sims can also be used to make labs—places for users to safely experiment with actions. The mechanics of the world are predictable and respond immediately to user decisions. Often, switches can be turned on or off, or dials up or down, with observable effects (Chapter 18).

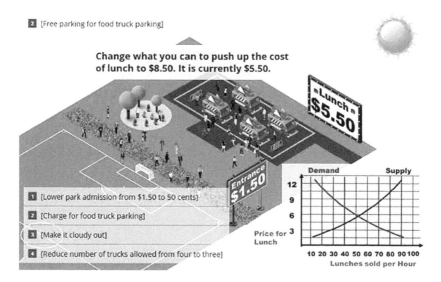

Short Sim as a Sandbox-Style Lab

Show Complex Processes

Some Short Sim help players follow and apply complex processes. Too often, traditional non-interactive methodologies have been painfully insufficient here. In schools, we have all experienced situations where a professor explained a mathematical process in a class, going through all of the steps, but even those of us who thought we were understanding the lecture were then dazzled later when faced with homework problems. Through chaperoned walk-throughs with dozens of small or abstracted decisions, Short Sims can eliminate this chasm between presented walk-throughs and competence in large organizations as well as schools (Chapter 17).

Allow Exploration of Interesting Systems

Short Sims may provide a sandbox for users to play in and see what happens. These explorations, often with goals or restraints, can be similar to labs, but include more social or business situations, and more complex and less predictable responses to actions. In one sandbox, a student runs a restaurant chain, but has to grow it through making only five decisions, with each opening up or closing down other opportunities. Different decisions result in very different endings which, along with the short play time, encourages trying again. The learning goal of this sim was to help employees adopt the perspective of a business owner and understand the strategic impact payment systems could make on a business' evolution. Sims that allow the exploration of interesting systems can be too unstructured for some students, and work best for MBA or military cultures, including high potential employees, with some kind of self-paced or group reflection or after action review (Chapter 15).

Short Sims Allow Explorations of Initially Non-Intuitive Systems

Present Complex Role Plays

Short Sims can be used to model complex role-plays between multiple people and agendas, and often feature visualizations of interpersonal dynamics. More complex sims have a richer "memory," and earlier decisions have an enduring impact throughout. This is in comparison with more simple sims, where often "what happens in level 2, stays in level 2." (Chapter 13).

Of course, just as a horror movie may still use humorous moments, almost all Short Sims draw on a variety of methods from different categories. The most engaging Short Sims, short or long, will all draw from the full tapestry of techniques, including those shown in the next few chapters.

10

Coaches, Settings, and the Value of Efficiency

It is now time to go into a bit more detail about some of the elements that have been introduced so far.

Often, a Coach

The Emmys and Oscars have hosts. These people set the tone, welcome the audience, and move things along. Similarly, many Short Sims should be designed with coaches. While also avatars, they serve a completely different role than the characters in sims.

Perhaps a better analogy for a coach in a sim is the acting instructor in a scene study workshop. The coach can discuss theory with the player, set up a role-play, end it, and even interrupt it to add new wrinkles. A coach can narrate impacts, good or bad, of decisions. The coach can, at any time in a scene, break the fourth wall and have a discussion with the player. The coach can even take on a character in a scenario or help the player achieve a goal by doing some menial tasks.

The coach, left, in an Army Short Sim, can step in and annotate a situation

Appendix 1 "Text Style Guide" shows how to punctuate these different coach roles to make it seamless for the player. But designers also need to get the tone right for the coach. I tend towards the Jarvis/Friday or Jeeves characters from Iron Man and Bertie fame, respectively. The coach is both smarter than the player and can present any hard rules, but also willing to go along with the player and let the player make mistakes. In this latter cases, the coach should say (or better, show), something like, "Your approach was not successful in meeting your goals," rather than, "You are wrong." The leadership style is collaborative, not directive.

For some sims, I like giving the coach a slight human weakness of some kind. I gave one coach a slight anger issue on which she was working. (Allowing the player to annoy the coach, breaking them out of their Socratic perfection, is always fun.) I made another coach sycophantic towards the player. One coach clearly did not want to be there. As with all humor, the goal is to be so dry that a player is hardly aware of it.

Coaches should never be referred to explicitly; the player should never say, for example, "Hey coach, why did half of my team quit?" saying instead just "Why did half of my team quit?" One test is your ability to remove the coach avatar and still have everything flow. (This is useful, because some clients decide they do not want to show a coach.)

Here is an example of a coachless coach:

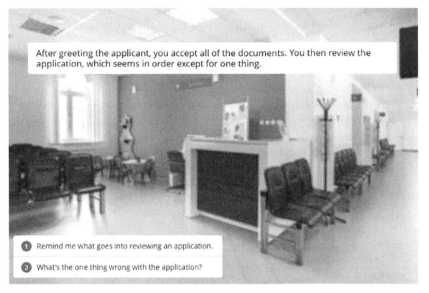

After greeting the applicant, you accept all of the documents. You then review the application, which seems in order except for one thing.

1 Remind me what goes into reviewing an application.

2 What's the one thing wrong with the application?

In this sim that this moment is from, the coach is not visualized through an avatar, yet still plays the typical coach roles, including setups, transitions, and feedback. The player has options that still are conversational.

On rare occasions, it is a challenge of a coach to find the right art. Some organizations can be a bit twitchy when it comes to committing to any single face of a program. However while, in designing sims, I have never included a coach and wished I had not, I have on occasion not included a coach and wished I had.

Creating Situations and Characters

Sims, with a coach or without, happen in a situation. Coming up with the right situation, a step which occurs after the initial research and decision around type, is often the first real decision in the design of the Short Sim.

And the situation of a sim is often the single most important decision in the design process as well. The right situation does a tremendous amount of pedagogical heavy lifting, in the best cases making the content self-evident.

If one has robust interview notes (from Chapter 6), use them to inform your situation, especially the three categories of Starting Points/Types of Challenges, Successful Outcomes, and Unsuccessful Outcomes.

Some sim situations are simple experiments, but most involve settings, characters, and narratives. Examples from this book include

- For the Be a Hacker sim, the situation put the player in the position of, you guessed it, a hacker.
- For the Play with Demand sim, in Chapter 13, the situation was giving the player control over the price of drinks in a food truck, with people in line visualizing the demand, and weather being the factor to show the shifts in demand curves. This was a very hard working setting, quite a bit of learning happens quickly, immediately, and without effort on the part of the learner.
- For the Credit Card company's case study sim shown in Chapter 22, the setting was a small company poised to grow and evolve.
- Any given slide should efficiently cover ground.

Here is an example of another setup:

This text (combined here from two subsequent screens) establishes the instigating event (acquired company, new job), the type of person the character is (people person), the character's challenge (creating new and legacy apps), and the player's relationship to the character (long-time acquaintance).

Consider Bare Stories

While situations are critical, stories in sims can be a bit of a trap. Stories that are too long or involved or specific can hurt the development process. Their construction too often results in endless stakeholder conversations and modifications, and the final story actually shortens the productive life of Short Sims considerably. They distract, not add to the learning. The answer instead is to keep them as lean as possible. Short Sim design aligns with the truism "less is more." The mini-levels in the first sim in Chapter 11 show an example of a central narrative introducing five different settings with just a sentence or two each.

Also Keep All Names Descriptive and Back-Stories Lean

Part of making stories lean is streamlining the names and histories of companies and characters. This makes players happier, as it reduces their cognitive load.
  Specifically,

- Minimize any unnecessary backstory; use variations of amalgamations of well-understood companies where possible. Use the business case study tradition of "Big Search" for a Google-like company, "Temp Workers Inc.," or "SportsWear Corp."
- Use character positions either instead of, or alongside, names. So use "Jack Jones, the defense lawyer" or just "the defense lawyer" every time the character is used, rather than introducing Jack Jones at the beginning and expecting people to remember him.

Consider Strong Characters

As an aside, don't use "less is more" as an excuse to make characters bland. In fact, characters with personalities are often critical to efficiency, doing a lot of heavy lifting in creating good experiences.

My goal is to establish a character in just a few words. For example, what does an avatar say when entering a room? It can vary from "Did anyone else see the spectacular sunrise today," to "Mondays make me wish I was dead," to "I have a meeting in Brussels tomorrow. I wonder if anyone would notice if I didn't show up?"

I keep copies of some Hollywood scripts, including James L. Brooks' *Broadcast News*, alongside more pedagogically focused books for inspiration. One writing trick I use is the equivalent of a scratch track character. Find a photograph of an interesting television or movie (or real world) character and put that in as one of the onscreen characters. Write dialogue aligned with that character. Then, just replace the visuals of the character before showing it.

A Commitment to Efficiency

Even though the approach of "less is more" aligns players and designers, it can initially be at odds with program sponsors. I have found that most learning organizations, when discussing serious games and educational simulations, will continue to add shiny features until they can no longer afford the money or time to produce it. So the discipline of ruthless efficiency, respecting the time of the students and the designer, must influence decisions in all aspects of production.

Minimize the Creation of Customized Media

For example, in making Short Sims, also shy away from customized sound or video. Use static images instead. And for those images, where pedagogically necessary, create custom art, but use clip art as a default.

This approach gets us important gains, beyond just cost.

- It increases flexibility. It allows designers to constantly add or change moments to increase comprehension and flow. The resulting experience is much smoother.
- It also reduces time. Every recorded voice, for example, represents many decisions that all eat up time and client attention, and has minimal pedagogical value.
- Translations are easier.
- Updates a year later are possible.

Further, as with elaborate stories, custom art can even hurt the sim. For example, there are times when a prop can be too specific. So, in our passport examples, if a process step is to collect a driver's license to see the age of a young applicant, using a mocked-up photograph of a driver's license may introduce two problems.

- First, because it would be from one specific state, it would be discordant with learners from other states.
- Second, because it would show a fixed date, the age of the applicant would increase in real time as subsequent learners played the sim.

An alternative to the photograph is a coach saying, "You take the driver's license, and you see from the date that the applicant is sixteen years old."

Use Alternative Text Characters (Judiciously) to Add Emphasis

The relentless quest for lean, effective design can turn up some surprising tools. Text-based windows can often accept certain alternative characters, which can be used to add emphasis and variety.

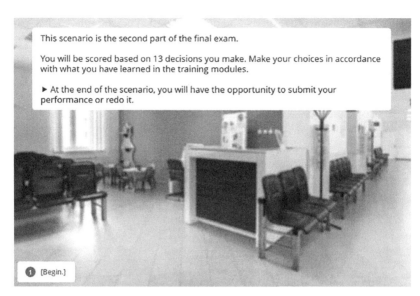

Alternative characters can be used for emphasis in most text windows.

Use as Few Words as Possible

One of the most important techniques is to, throughout your process, gain efficiency for you and your players by always using as few words as possible. Be almost (old) Twitter like in the restrictions on characters used. Let the interactions do the pedagogical heavy lifting. (And yes, it initially takes more time to write more leanly, but you will save the time on updates.)

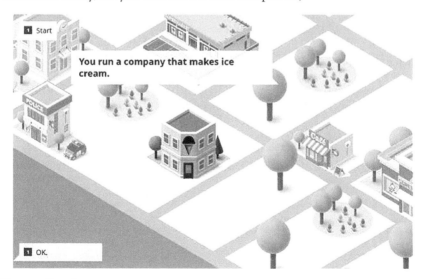

Few words redux

This also means using the responses to do some work. For example, in this introduction to a sim, the setup and the responses are used together to convey the necessary material.

There are three parts, which you can go through in any order. Where would you like to go?

1 Got it.

1 Part One: The Family
2 Part Two: Change in Plans
3 Part Three: 15 and Under

The user options can be used to convey information.

Efficient Structures

And finally, always strive for efficient structures. Some new designers are proud of their giant, sprawling sim designs. But more experienced designers know that there is value in a smaller and tighter sim structure. This makes changes easier for you to make and any future authors.

Useful Across All Types

These approaches are useful in all Short Sim types, including inculcating new ways of thinking, which will be the focus of the next chapter.

Examples of Inculcating New Ways of Thinking

Short Sims can be designed to create transformation thoughts and other new ways for players to think about their world. There are at least two ways of doing this. One way is to get the player to fail using an old mindset, which we will discuss in Chapter 14. A second way is to create a new starting point.

Creating a New Starting Point

There is the old joke of a Boston couple driving up to a Maine farmer and asking for directions to Portland. The farmer thinks for a moment and say "Well, if I were you, I wouldn't start from here."

This is an important Short Sim opportunity—to present some microcosm or analogy that circumvents preconceptions. For example, one topic of traditional Econ 101 is *international trade*. Counter intuitively to modern students, Adam Smith's model is not one of zero-sum negotiating but of each country focusing on where they have what is called "comparative advantage." To ease the students into this way of thinking, this first sim in the series presents a collaborative relationship between two housemates who are figuring out how to best share the chores.

There is not the giant lightbulb of the Be a Hacker sim but creates a quickly gained comfort in the right way of thinking.

- Go to level directly here: www.shortsims.com/ch11

Storyboard (Spoilers)

For those who cannot play the sim, here are some interactions.

The setup for the sim is simple:

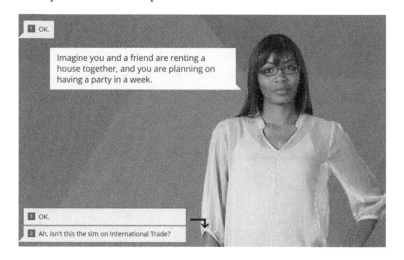

The sim then presents a series of six connected questions, starting with this one:

1 OK...?

Here is what each of you can do in two hours. Who should do what to be the most productive?

	Decorate		Earn
You	3 Rooms	or	$20
Housemate	2 Rooms	or	$10

1 It is more productive if I decorate 3 rooms and my housemate earns $10.

2 It is more productive if my housemate decorates 2 rooms and I earn $20.

3 I am not sure how to think about this.

Some of the questions introduce concepts, such as the third question, shown in the Preface of this book, which is on opportunity costs.

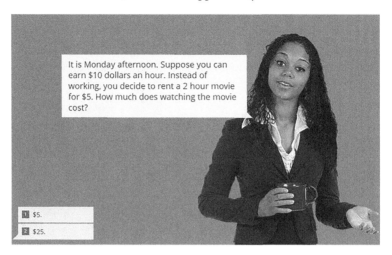

This is a satisfying example of a question that is not asked because it is hard, but because in the process of having to answer it—and only giving two possible answers—the user has to create for themselves a theory of opportunity cost that they will need to better understand the next questions. This happens in less than twenty seconds and without much effort.

The fourth question provides the setup of, "For the party, you and your housemate need rooms decorated and there is a chance to earn money for food." Then, it asks

1 OK.

You and your housemate will go together for errands. Your housemate is local and drives more efficiently. Who should drive?

	Get to		
You	4 Stores	*in*	2 Hours
Housemate	5 Stores	*in*	2 Hours

1 My housemate will drive. I will be the passenger.

2 I will drive. My housemate will be the passenger.

The final set of questions zooms into the heart of the new way of thinking, which has been prepared through the earlier questions.

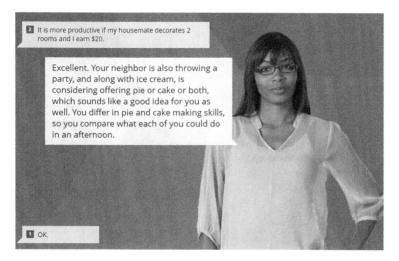

The thinking, even the way that the answers are presented, nudges the user further along the path. This level does require a bit more internalizing of concepts.

1 OK.

Assuming a fair trade so you will both have a variety, who should make the cakes? (Hint: If a slice of pie is worth a dollar, who gives up the least money to make 50 servings of cake?)

	Pie		Cake
You	20 Servings	*or*	50 Servings
Neighbor	15 Servings	*or*	50 Servings

1 I should. If I make cake, it will cost me the $20 worth of pie I could have made."

2 My neighbor should. It will only cost my neighbor $15 worth of pie.

3 What would the exchange rate be in this scenario?

The sim ends with a final example that complete the transitions to international trade.

Techniques of Note

This *International Trade, Part 1* Short Sim uses a few favorite techniques, including:

- It uses level design, taking the player along a smooth *learning curve*. The first problem presented is ridiculously easy. This gets the player comfortable with the interface. Then, it takes the users through incrementally more challenging comparisons, while keeping the simplicity of the binary choices. Players teach themselves the content. Learning curves are present in all Short Sim examples in this book and explained a bit more explicitly in Chapters 12 and 16.
- Sims can easily expose players to many variations of similar content over a short period of time. These practice sessions build a higher comfort level.
- The sudden death effect (if a player gets a single wrong answer, the sim starts over) adds some drama, but never in a way that gets too tense.

Our housemate/party scenario has a series of math problems wrapped in short situations. Each math problem is a mini-scenario and a mini-level. The connecting narrative of housemates planning a party establishes a non-competitive relationship, critical to understanding the real topic. The overall tone is non-stressful. The slight story is sufficient for the material to go down smoothly, without binding and chaffing (too much) along the way. Of course as obvious as the story seems in retrospect, it took an hour or so of mulling to come up with it. The better the design, alas, the more it seems effortless and inevitable.

Example: Combining New Way of Thinking and Predictable Process

Some Short Sims combine techniques. This second sim example, On Utility, <www.shortsims.com/ch11> has three levels. The structure of each level is

1. A *new way of thinking* at the beginning
2. Some explanation of theory
3. A *process application level* (at the end of the sim) from this chapter.

It is around the dreaded Econ 101 concept of marginal utility.

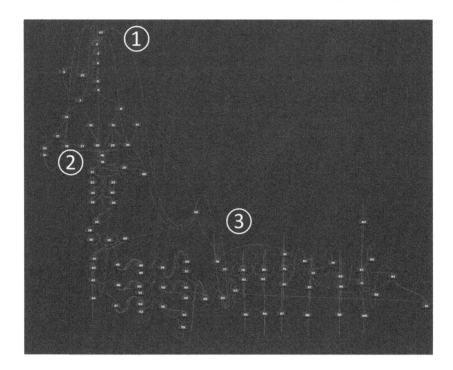

The flow chart behind "On Utility," identifying the start of each of the segments.

The pedagogy around level design, including this one, will be expanded upon next chapter.

12

On Levels

Short Sims are made up of levels. One nine-minute Short Sim may have as many as six or eight distinct segments. And most levels should have at least one *moment of truth* decision, but more likely three. The average number of screens for a level is about fourteen. For background, if you haven't already, consider playing the second sim—the three level sim—from the last chapter, and look at the picture of its underlying structure.

Or consider a leadership sim, where a manager has to check in with five employees on a Monday morning. Likely, the sim would have at least five levels, one for each employee.

In other cases, levels can break up distinct activities in a process. A veterinarian may have several activities that make up her afternoon, each with opportunities for success or failure. Ideally, the levels collectively create a mood or atmosphere that pay off or otherwise impact the final, and often most important, actions.

Levels are like sections in a paper or book. They should segue from one to another seamlessly, with transitions such as this one from a conversation with an intern (Level 1) to an examination (Level 2):

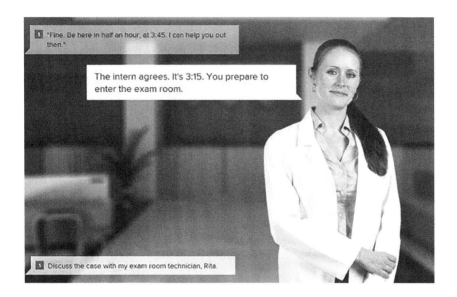

A seamless "level" transition from a conversation with an intern to an examination.

The Zen of Level 1

The first level should introduce an example of the type of interactivity the user can expect throughout the short sim, but in a simple and self-evident implementation. The user should not be able to fail the first level no matter what, but there should still be some opportunity to try different things if the user so desires.

From a planning and architecture perspective, however, while early levels should be simpler for the player, they may take more scaffolding and hand holding, and so may be more complex and time-consuming to design and build than later levels. Give the player chances to ask questions, be snarky, and otherwise play with the interface.

Using Bottlenecks (i.e., What Happens in Level 3, Stays in Level 3)

A second useful rule of thumb for levels is independence. In most cases, levels in Short Sims should not affect each other. From a design perspective, this means that the connections between levels are a bottleneck (i.e., a single link connects the end of one level to the beginning of the next). This greatly simplifies creation and testing, as each level can be built in isolation. In more than a few occasions, part of the last-minute massaging of the content involves switching the order of some of the later levels for narrative or skill building purposes, which should be fairly easy in this kind of project.

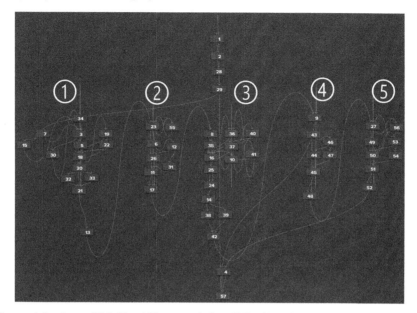

The architecture of this Short Sim reveals five distinct levels.

Create a Few Traps

FYI, one situation that should haunt all designers is that their Short Sim is put in front of a CEO, who then bangs randomly on keys without paying attention, and ends up with a good conclusion. There should be some minilabs that catch this, which are a few interactions that, if clicked mindlessly, result in either a failure or a loop.

A Learning Curve

To riff off Archimedes, "Give me a some interactivity and a shallow enough learning curve, and I can teach anyone anything."

When designing Short Sims, we need to master the application of learning curves, the technique of slightly increasing the difficulty over many turns, with feedback, to build competence and conviction.

Chapter 13's case study provides an example of implementing a learning curve. Chapter 16 provides two more examples to study.

What follows is one more example (in appendix level detail), which most readers should skip, but practioners may find interesting.

Here is an example of a sim about a predictable process that uses a slightly unconventional interface with a rigorous level design:

Specifically, returning to a touchstone topic of this book, this Short Sim on accepting a passport application built a comfort with some of the math involved:

1. The coach sets up the situation.

2. The coach presents the details.

3. Rather than being thrown into a sea of numbers, the player is eased in by the coach. This level design—with the first few decisions being very simple—is also typical of casual computer games. Importantly, the coach takes on a helpful tone, volunteering to keep a running total, and using expressions such as "let us figure out...."

4. If the player had chosen Passport Card (which the player did not in this situation), the following explanation would have been presented.

5. But the player got this question right. And again, early on in the sequence, to ease any number phobia, the player's decisions are around what influences the numbers, not the numbers themselves.

6. Help is made available so that the player can learn more on the fly, but does not have to.

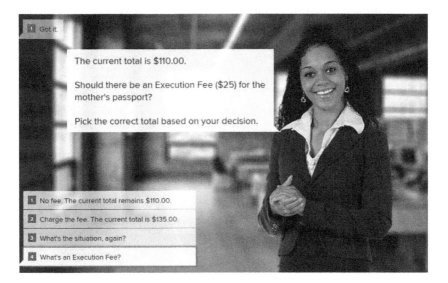

7. The "help" fully answers the question.

8. There is also always a button for the player to be reminded what the situation is to help with the decisions.

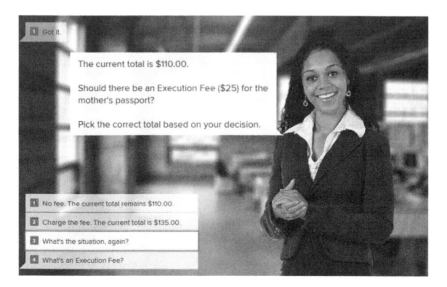

9. The situation reminder provides the rest of the necessary information. Again, it is not proactively presented to the player, but has to be asked for, streamlining the experience.

10. We now return to where we had been. Short Sims, such as this one, can present quite a few easy questions in a short time to build comfort and experience, not just one big hard question to trick and test the player.

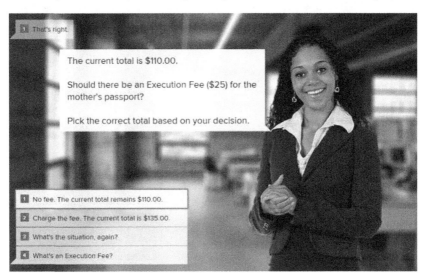

11. Often, information is presented through the player's possible answers, so the player can feel smart while the program is doing the explicit teaching.

12. This next sequence requires the application of a variation of what the player has learned.

13. Subtly, the problems get harder, and now the player has to both make the decision and perform the math to answer.

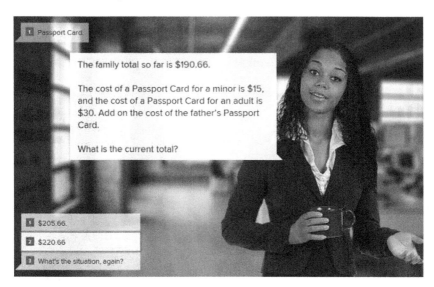

14. Again, the player has to make the decision and do the math to answer.

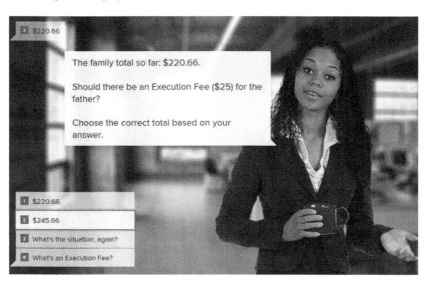

15. One more simple question:

16. The final pricing is for the daughter, which is a third variation because she is a minor.

17. Here, answering the question again requires the execution of a typical math problem, to gently raise comfort.

18. By the end of this two-minute sequence, the player understands what it is like to experience the level of math necessary to accept applications, gained some confidence in variations, and even has experienced what the final totals may look like. From a design perspective, the entire experience does not require custom art, and so is easy to change at any moment when passport fees are changed.

In some cases, a disciplined player may complete this level but still want to go through it a second or even third time to build more comfort.

Make Sure Players Know, When They Failed, Why. Exactly

Whenever a player fails, make sure he or she understands why the path was wrong.

Specifically, when a player arrives at a negative outcome, show the player why. Allow the player to experience emotionally the direct negative consequences. Visualize the "invisible system," which is the flow of events that people can't normally see, but leads to problems.

For example, consider a cybersecurity sim.

Do not just say:

You fail. Putting the thumb drive in the computer is a violation of IA Policy 17,543b.

Instead say (perhaps with an illustrations):

When any thumb drive is put into a USB port, it auto-runs a small program. Unknown to you, the thumb drive had been infected with a worm during the manufacturing process that had not yet been identified by a major anti-virus company. This time, the virus was able to infect the local computer and then, two days later, the server. Within a week, the virus had spread to not just local computers but remote computers as well. A group of mobsters in a foreign country was able to access passwords and then other mission critical information, which they sold for two thousand dollars to a foreign government.

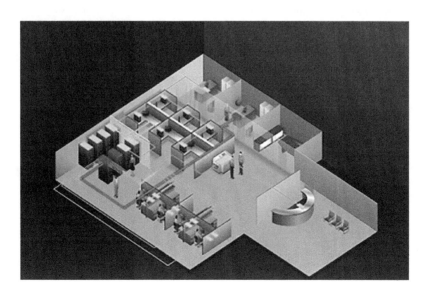

Illustrations can be useful.

Then, of course, allow the player to try again.

Here is an example from a Passport acceptance center, showing the consequences of not asking the applicant to write all of the names on an application check.

1 [Accept both checks as is.]

You finish, and package up the five applications and the Department of State check. However, the applications get split up in processing. Two are sent to one agency, and three are sent to a different one.

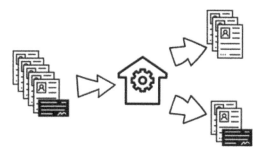

1 [Continue.]

1 [Continue.]

One of the two passport processing centers gets an applicant's check that is for too large for the products described.

Because there are no annotations on the check, such as the names of the applicants for whom the check covers, there are many different possibilities the processing center has to consider.

1 [Continue.]

1 [Continue.]

The passport center has to consider if the applicant is expecting time-critical services, such as expedited processing.

1 [Continue.]

1 [Continue.]

At the same time, the rest of the applications arrive at one center without any payment. This results in a rejection letter being sent to the applying family.

1 OK.

1 OK.

Try going back and asking the mother or father to write all of the names on the memo field of the one check.

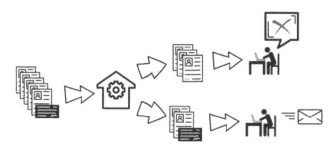

1 OK.

Players should never make the same mistake twice, if a sim is designed well. In fact, the player should leave the sim being a rabid supporter of any relevant rules. This is how branching stories can build true conviction.

Decisions Should Have Stakes

Use emotional consequences if they are part of showing why a mistake is a mistake.

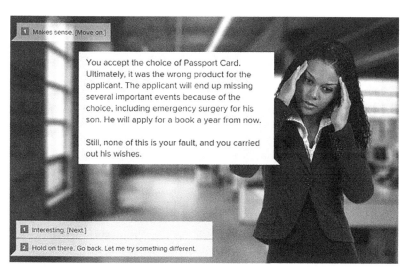

1 Makes sense. [Move on.]

You accept the choice of Passport Card. Ultimately, it was the wrong product for the applicant. The applicant will end up missing several important events because of the choice, including emergency surgery for his son. He will apply for a book a year from now.

Still, none of this is your fault, and you carried out his wishes.

1 Interesting. [Next.]

2 Hold on there. Go back. Let me try something different.

Decisions should have stakes.

Be Cautious When Presenting "Wrong Answers" Not to Reinforce a Mistake

Sims give players the opportunities to make mistakes. And the heightened emotions of decision making are one reason they work so well. However, I sometimes take steps to make sure I am not introducing worst practices when presenting possible wrong answers.

Here is an example, continuing with one of our case studies. Passport photographs are rejected if the applicant's hair is covering the eyes, but are fine if the hair covers the ears. One mistake that agents make in the real world is rejecting a photograph for the latter reason.

So we may create a setup that looks like this:

You look at the photograph.

① The photograph is acceptable.

② The photograph is unacceptable.

③ [Ask the applicant a question.]

④ [Use the photo guide.]

This will be a two-part interface, where the first part is a broad identification of a problem. We will then follow up with a request of the player to identify the specific reason.

We as designers now have to identify what reasons we can present, typically one right and the rest wrong. We can use this opportunity to reinforce possible reasons for rejecting a photograph, such as "the wrong distance between the applicant and the camera," even if they do not apply to this specific situation.

But how should we catch the common mistake identified by our expert of rejecting a photograph because the ears are covered? What would you do? How would you write the text for that response?

The obvious approach, giving the player the wrong answer of "Ears are covered," turns out to be a bad idea. Even if they clicked on it, and would be told there is no problem with ears being covered, it may potentially reinforces a wrong idea. The player may remember the phrase without remembering if it was the right or wrong thing to do. Instead, I used a broader concept that was accurate, but that would be wrongly applied in this situation (below).

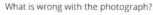
What is wrong with the photograph?

1. Bad lighting.

2. The wrong distance between the applicant and the camera.

3. Key portions of the face are covered.

4. Change my answer to [The photograph is acceptable.]

The wrong answer of "Key portions of the face are covered" is nevertheless a real reason that some passport photographs are rejected, and the answer here would catch the misconception of "hair should not cover the ears" without explicitly presenting inaccurate statement. This consideration is not always possible to apply, but it is useful to think about.

Balancing Lecture and Lab: On the Philosophy of Right Seat and Left Seat

The U.S. military has a concept called "right seat and left seat" learning, which may be worth borrowing for developing competence. When a new soldier arrives at a post, he or she may shadow someone with more experience to get the lay of the land and understand what the new assignment entails. The new soldier first rides in the right seat—the passenger seat—of the vehicle to watch the expert. Then, when the new soldier understands a bit more, he or she may switch to the left side—the driver's side—and start performing the job, but with mentoring from the more experienced person, who is now in the passenger seat. Finally, the mentor can leave completely.

Short Sims have to develop both right seat and left seat learning. This can mean switching between instruction and experience. The demand curve sim in the next chapter is a good example of balancing the two.

Be Player-Centric

As one creates levels, it is always useful to remember that the center of the design universe is the player. Here are some additional techniques for the user interface:

Keep the Player Active by Breaking Up Long Passages

My goal is to keep the metronome of user engagement predictably brisk. I try to avoid situations where the player has to read or hear more than three sentences before performing some activity.

Don't Break the Player's Flow

One wants to create a sim where the player can play a version of themselves, or some plausible alternative reality version of themselves. Or a smarter version of themselves.

Consider this typical setup the player is in a situation where the character that they are playing meets a friend for the first time in a decade.

It may be fun to write, "How the heck are you? How's it hanging?" However, most people would be uncomfortable saying that, and would disconnect from the sim the moment they were *forced* to say it. One alternative, then, would be to write the more conservative, "Hello, Tim, it is good to see you again." However, in some cultures, there is no reason not to give both options, to allow for the fun and energy of the first option (which may warrant a different reaction but in no other way impact the narrative) alongside the more conservative answer.

One can even be more generic and present two intention options as "[Greet friend warmly.]" or "[Greet friend neutrally.]." For more grammar, see the Text Style Guide in Appendix 1.

One can even combine the two, with

- [Greet friend warmly] "How the heck are you?"
- [Greet friend] "Hello, Tim, it is good to see you again."

In other situations, it is pedagogically useful to make the player smarter than he or she is in real life. For example,

Your friend asks you what kind of shirt to buy.

- "Try the West Indian Sea Island Cotton, with the hand pointed collar."
- "Try the two-fold 120 blue cotton shirt with regent collar and smart double cuffs."
- Tell me more about the two shirts.

The last option is spoken to the coach, thus the lack of quotation marks. A variation is to, first, give the player control of the intention. To the question above,

- [Suggest a more casual shirt.]
- [Suggest a more formal shirt.]
- Tell me more about the two shirts.

Then, have the coach, on the next screen, appear and (with the second example) say, "You tell your friend to try the try the two-fold 120 blue cotton shirt with regent collar and smart double cuffs. You also point out the mother-of-pearl buttons." Then, have the player acknowledge with a "Makes sense."

This "player, but smarter" approach has a tremendous pedagogical payoff. The players read the information carefully when deciding which option to make. It also offloads text from the setup description, keeping that lean. It is also simply more fun to play a smarter version of yourself.

This desire to not to break the player's buy-in within the simulation section still allows for a coach to break the fourth wall. As said earlier, the mood created for the learner should be similar to an actor in a drama workshop, who switches between being a character invested in a scene and a student learning from a guide.

13

Case Study

Creating a Short Sim Lab on Demand Curves

Short Sims can also be used to make labs—places for users to safely experiment. This is a brief walk-through of the process of creating such a Short Sim to be embedded in a college textbook. The example is simple, yet required several useful techniques.

Introduction

The Bill and Melinda Gates Foundation funded a collection of open source textbooks on popular community college topics. For their Econ 101 series, I was asked to create dozens of Short Sims, each about five to ten minutes long.

Our strategy was to use sims in these electronic textbooks earlier on for foundational areas and later for more challenging areas. The first sim was to cover an introduction to demand curves.

Before going further, play the five-minute Short Sim for yourself:

- *Link*: www.shortsims.com/ch13

Understand the Topic and the Objectives for the Short Sim

The first thing I had to do, as designer, was understand the topic. In this case, content was widely available. Generic online research was sufficient.

Still, some conversations with experts were useful. One professor helped me immensely with the comment, "many econ students end up thinking the visualization of a demand curve is a static icon of the topic, not something dynamic."

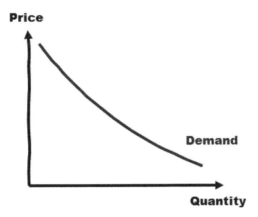

A Demand Curve

Note: When topics requires organization specific or even proprietary content, research takes significantly longer.

Create a Visual and Intuitive Microcosm

Given the subject matter, there were numerous ways I could have structured the sim.

One early design decision had to be centered on what to do with the *visual* of a demand curve. Should it be the biggest visual element on the screen? I didn't think so. In the real world, a demand curve should serve in a helper role, a tool for better understanding the productive world, so that is the path I chose to follow. I wanted to create a situation where understanding the demand curve was of actual help in accomplishing another goal, not the end goal. I wanted students to want the demand curve.

For this situation, I honed in on the framing activity of pricing drinks, with food trucks for the microcosm. For this sim—and the next few in the series—food trucks became a hard-working situation. They could show a fluid marketplace as described by economist Adam Smith, while still be fast-paced enough to be relatable to a modern student.

Food trucks also made visualization easy. The number of people in line could intuitively show demand, while more trucks showing up at an event, for example, could represent greater supply. As with all sims, the more I could create situations where the students taught themselves, the better.

It may be relevant to note here that I cannot draw. On the bigger sims for which I am the lead designer, I work with real artists and animators. But my challenge here was to role model an approach that could be done by one individual, to make the project both cost-effective and, more importantly, easy to change when the need arose. At the same time, the effect had to be the kind of satisfying and intuitive interactivity from which a player could observe cause and effect in real time.

A Simple, Clean Presentation

As a place-holder, I decided on a visual style of simple, black-and-white graphics, completely assembled using clip-art in PowerPoint. Shadows made it easier to count. In this initial version, I even created personalities for those in line, where the thirstiest people (sweat emanating) and wealthiest (bags of money, top hat) could hang on longer as the price went up. This was never to be discussed explicitly in the sim, but I figured it could be explored by an ambitious instructor. I try to put in quite a few Easter eggs in every sim for users to discover, just as I try to leave out a bit of pedagogical information for any instructor, if there is one, to impart.

To meet the learning objectives for this sim, I also had to figure out how to cover *shifts in demand curves*. (*Shifts* refer to how the demand curve graph can move one way or another, left or right, based on external changing conditions.) I settled on a *cloudy day* versus *sunny*. To mangle *The Art of War*, the best way to explain something is to create a situation where you do not have to explain it at all.

A Few Actions and a Simple Interface

The actual interactivity—the user actions—would then be around raising and lowering the prices for a drink, and also changing the condition from sunny to cloudy. This provided a simple three-button interface that could take a user through a wide range of conditions. Feedback—the changes in the scene—could be immediate and calibrated.

Level One: The Introduction to the Lab

It made sense to build the Short Sim with two levels. The first level had to introduce the content and key functionality as elegantly and effortlessly as possible.

(Isometric graphics would replace the black-and-white versions, and became a consistent look and feel for many of the Econ 101 sims.)

Introduce Interactivity

This first Short Sim level had to develop a comfort with the four options of

- Advance/Make choices with implication
- Raise drink prices
- Lower drink prices
- Change the weather, from sunny to cloudy, or cloudy to sunny.

The design goal was to introduce these actions one at a time. Users had to demonstrate some basic facility in order to advance to the next one.

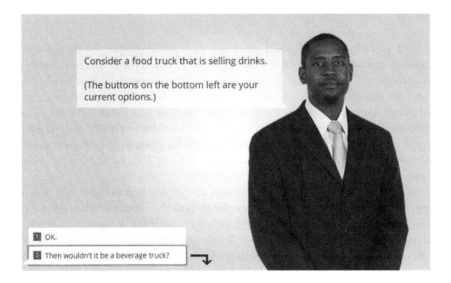

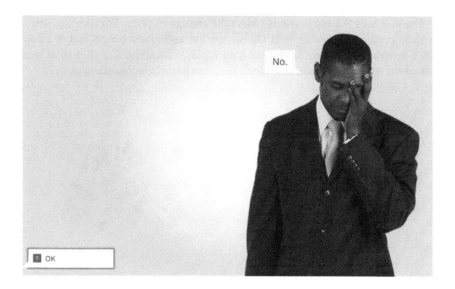

Here is an early moment from the demand sim introducing the basic advance button, with a simple choice (and a concomitant sense of mild responsiveness to the choice made).

Note: In general, I like giving the user the opportunity to talk back a bit (or more) to the onscreen avatar, to vent any rebellious streak, and get a bit of feedback for it. These paths are always optional, of course. But they also serve as interface practice, so should be included if possible.

The following sequence, a few screens later, introduces the ability to raise prices and a few other sim elements:

The price is now $1.00. Keep going. Raise the price now to $1.50.

1 [Lower the price by $0.50.]

2 [Raise the price by $0.50.]

The user sees the big marquis reflect the change in price. Phrases like "throw in some customers" are meant to lower tension and give a breezy feel of a computer-generated sandbox, with play (and replay) encouraged, rather than some real-world situations where the wrong decision has dire consequences.

Good job. Let's throw in some customers. As with the real world, these customers are price sensitive.

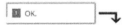

There is a constant effort to minimize words. Now, we introduce both the line of customers as a representation of demand and the helpful demand curve graphic.

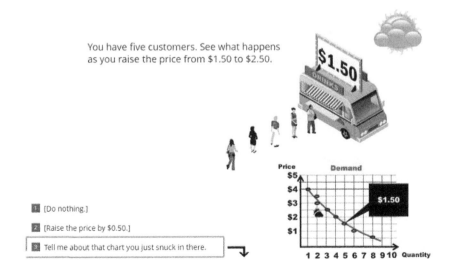

You have five customers. See what happens as you raise the price from $1.50 to $2.50.

1 [Do nothing.]

2 [Raise the price by $0.50.]

3 Tell me about that chart you just snuck in there.

We do not force the user to learn explicitly about the demand curve. Instead, we do the opposite. We make the user have to decide they want to know more about it.

I like making users ask for information. The decision to ask makes the information more valuable and better received, and allows the students the role of being virtuous. For comparison, the same customer in a restaurant may be upset when the sandwich they ordered arrived unexpectedly with whole wheat bread, but feel virtuous if they ordered it that way. It also greatly increases a Short Sim design objective of replayability.

Typically older users will want all of the information beforehand, while the younger will charge ahead. We don't have to choose. A sim can present the same offer for information multiple times. This is one way that Short Sim can get a bit closer to the goal of personalized learning.

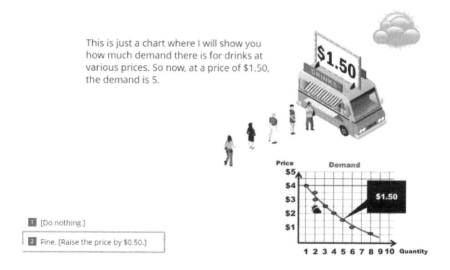

This is just a chart where I will show you how much demand there is for drinks at various prices. So now, at a price of $1.50, the demand is 5.

1 [Do nothing.]

2 Fine. [Raise the price by $0.50.]

Users could see the change in customers waiting when *they* raised the price, and also see how the demand curve represented it. (The screen responds to the *users* actions, which is a different and often more powerful than passive video.) The black box with the pointer arrow, a later pedagogical addition, created additional satisfying movement.

I then introduced the ability to change the weather in a similar manner. Users could see for themselves that more people would buy a drink at the same price on a hot day than overcast.

Note: I made the weather interface a simple toggle, which kept the buttons to three.

Vocabulary was introduced the same way, with a natural, repetitive use to create comfort. Also to encourage replayability, this part of the sim is easy for a player to breeze through, but can also be explored a bit.

Consistency

You may have noticed in the last screenshot above, an odd "Do nothing" option at the top of the multiple choice menu. Or not. Most users will not give it a second thought.

But this serves an important role. In fact, this gets at one of the most interesting, powerful, but surprising design principles in the entire book, that of *consistent interface*. (In academic parlance, yes, this will be on the test.)

From the earliest computer games, designers made sure that pushing up on the joystick always made your on screen character go up, and pushing down on the joystick always made your character go down. With that interface, after a few seconds of experimentation, players could get anywhere on the screen by making dozens of small "decisions" without thinking much about it.

Consistent Interface

If a sim asked the player to review a dozen words and identify which were spelled right, you would expect the "Spelled right" and "Spelled wrong" buttons always to be in the same place in relation to each other. The same one would always be on top, or on the left, for example. This consistency should be applied wherever possible and especially when a lot of decisions have to be made in a row.

My goal is a similar *repetitive consistency*. If "Raise the price" of drinks is currently available in the sim, it is always option 2. So what does this have to do with the "Do nothing" option on the screen shot above?

In the early joystick example, pushing up on the joystick always made your on screen character go up. Except when there was a wall you were walking into. Or you hit the top of the screen. Or there was some instructional section that temporarily disable the "up" option. In these cases, the ability to go up simply stopped working for the moment.

For the lab in this demand curve sim—outside of talking to the coach—there are up to three commands available (shown below, left):

1 [Lower the price by $0.50.]　　　**1** [Do nothing.]

2 [Raise the price by $0.50.]　　　**2** [Raise the price by $0.50.]

3 [Wait for the sun to come out.]

However, because only one, "Raise the price," was available at that moment, the user was presented with a truncated list (shown above, right). This is the equivalent of our joystick using player running into a wall. Done well, it does not even raise an eyebrow, but reduces work on the part of the player.

I will use variations of this technique to maintain interface consistency on the full core lab as well described below.

By the way, the concept of striving for a consistent interface, implemented simply here, is one to which we will return often throughout this book to unpack all of the implications, including in the section in the next chapter called "Unforced Decisions." It opens up more possibilities than most designers first realize.

Level Two: The Core Lab

From here, I created the core lab. The user was to have a more open-ended and less chaperoned opportunity to engage the model. Some call this *sandbox-mode*.

I also had to create a victory condition towards which the player must strive. It could have been something easy and intuitive like "find the price and weather combination that results in the lowest possible demand." I chose instead to ask the player to find a very specific demand situation, which required a bit more experimentation.

The payoff for the consistent interface allowed the user to not have to focus on it at all. Oddly, many users actually enjoyed the process of repeatedly lowering or raising the price, just to see how the world reacted. This kind of soothing and plea-surable twitch activity, akin to throwing a basketball into a hoop or matching cards in solitaire, is necessary for a great game and certainly a bonus for this type of lab.

Here is a sequence.

Here, the user first raises the price of drinks by 50 cents:

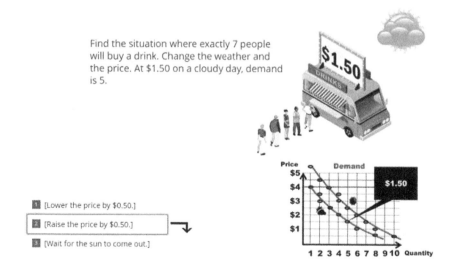

Find the situation where exactly 7 people will buy a drink. Change the weather and the price. At $1.50 on a cloudy day, demand is 5.

1 [Lower the price by $0.50.]

2 [Raise the price by $0.50.]

3 [Wait for the sun to come out.]

The demand line predictably shrinks from five to four. Then, the user changes the weather (or, to put it in user action terms, waits for the sun to come out) and sees what happens:

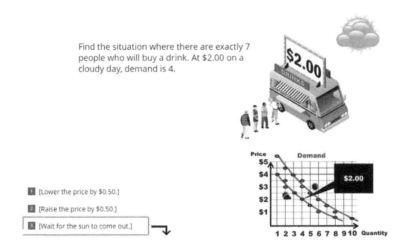

The black arrow moves, drawing attention to how the rise in temperature shifts the demand curve to the right. The user can experience that for the same price of $2.00, demand increases from 4 to 6. Some users will toggle the weather button again and again, just to see what happens and draw the appropriate conclusions. For the sake of visually impaired people, I put in brief descriptions that could be read by a screen reader. In this design, it is easier to present the current state ("At $2.00 on a sunny day, demand is six.") rather than describe the change ("Demand has increased from four to six."), but one could do both.

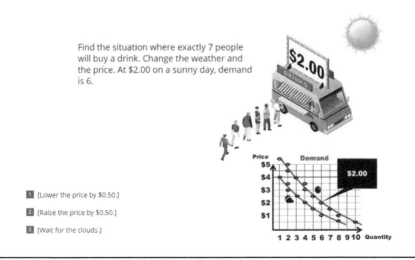

Virtually all users, with a bit of strategy and a bit of banging around, find the victory condition of seven people in line. The lab tells them when they are successful.

In our sim, the demand curve serves as a mini-map, akin the map on a driving game, providing a helpful and valued strategic view that aligned with what the player was doing and seeing. Multiple simultaneous views of the same, user-controlled situation help the user discover for themselves about demand curves.

Computer game genres routinely use mini-maps for a strategic view, including the classic *Midtown Madness*. © Microsoft Corporation

Most users would be upset if the demand curve was taken away, as it would make the activity much harder. This is, of course, the point.

Note: For the effect of dynamic and open-ended interactivity to be achieved in Level 2, 22 PowerPoint slides were created that reflected all possible permutations. The screenshot below (from tool BranchTrack) shows how they were wired, with two columns that matched the two demand curves shown on the chart. From any screen, the user could go up, down, or across, which corresponded with raising or lowering the price, or changing the sun/cloud situation. I find it critical to arrange the screens in a logical and helpful way, which makes later editing so much easier.

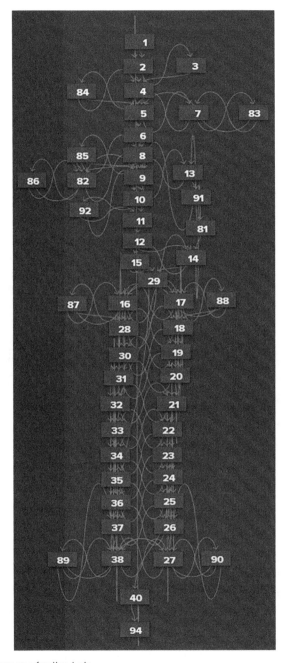

Twenty-two screens for the Lab

13. Case Study

This victory condition ("Find the situation where exactly seven people...") was repeated on every slide.

Here are two final thoughts.

On Tone and an Ideal Way to Learn

One area on which I obsess more than most is around tone. As discussed in Chapter 10, my favorite voice for the onscreen coach is of Jeeves or Jarvis—both gentleman's gentleman.

Specially, the coach is older, wiser, more of an adult, and the primary interface to the sim's challenges. This allows the user to be more impetuous, mischievous, experimental, and alternate between childish and brilliant.

The coach, as helper, can do some of the grunt work for the user and report back information. Here is a moment, an example from the next sim on supply curves:

The coach is there to serve.

As one is designing sims with this gentleman's gentleman perspective, the coach shouldn't contradict the wishes of the user directly, but can dissuade, and report back if something failed or is something is impossible, often with an implied deep and heartfelt sense of regret. The coach can subtly push the user towards a solid "good enough" solution, but also be surprised when the user pulls out some clever approach that works even better.

In this approach, there are many other actions possible. Later in the same supply sim, the coach tints the interface, while the user can bark out Stark-like commands:

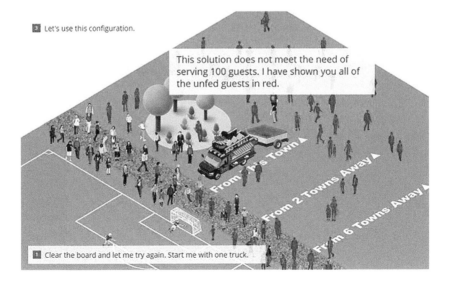

It may be ideal to learn in an interactive environment where we can do crazy things, with a chaperone ready to obey our orders, tirelessly pick up our pieces and do other grunt work, give us advice, couch any feedback, and ultimately keep us from going too far.

On Using PowerPoint and Borrowing from Comic Strips

As I mentioned, counter-intuitively to any actual graphic artist, I use PowerPoint as a tool to assemble the graphics and then export the graphics. This allowed speed and is surprisingly efficient for making many images with relatively small differences between them to create a sense of interactivity and responsiveness.

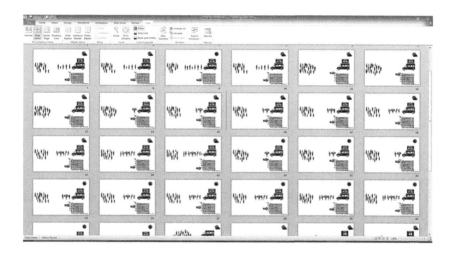

PowerPoint was used to assemble the clip-art graphics, with slide numbers corresponding to screen numbers in sim design. This is a bit tedious, but it allows one person with neither artistic nor technical skills to produce the sim. This maintained a flexibility throughout the process where just one person could quickly make updates as needed, which results in a more natural sim experience.

This approach allowed me to easily respond to the client request to change the graphic style from the two-dimensional graphics to a more isometric approach. This 3D look matched the other sims I was developing for them, but I was sorry to lose the personalities of the people waiting in line. I could relatively efficiently cut and paste over each original, and turn in the new version to the client in a very timely manner. In a more traditional project, I would have had to involve artists and rebuild scenes and do extensive debugging.

Also, as part of the graphics process, to overcome the limited affordances of static screens (and also for fun), I used techniques from comic strips or comic books when possible. In the screenshot below, I added motion lines to the two characters to support the idea they were walking away from the truck:

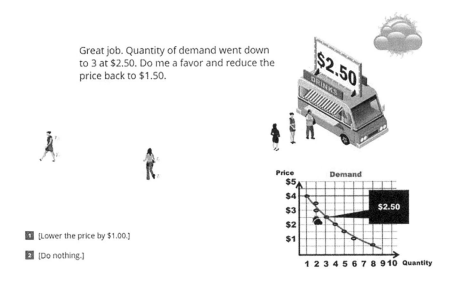

Great job. Quantity of demand went down to 3 at $2.50. Do me a favor and reduce the price back to $1.50.

1 [Lower the price by $1.00.]

2 [Do nothing.]

Conclusion

Many so far have found the sim to be an easy, engaging way to learn about demand curves, more quickly, more enjoyably, and with a richer understanding than other approaches. The information sticks because it is earned. It builds a more robust conviction, not just a brittle awareness.

All of this is accomplished in a Short Sim comprised of just 56 screens, some with graphics and some without, about two levels of gameplay, and tied together with a network of links.

14

Short Sim Example

Carpool (And Techniques to Align Behaviors in a Sim to Real-World Behaviors)

Overview

Play this *Carpool* sim.

- Link to Carpool: www.shortsims.com/ch14

This Carpool sim creates a situation that entices the player to make a bad choice that aligns with a real-world bad choice of a lot of people. To develop empathy, the player has to not act perfectly.

The Challenges and the Needs to Line Up with the Real World

Sims should model—at some abstract level—the real world. *This also means that players should make the same mistakes in the sim as they do or would in the productive world.*

This is often pedagogical necessity. When we ask experts about why real people make real mistakes in the real world in such areas as cybersecurity, ethics, leadership, corruption, maintenance, and sexual harassment, we hear: "they have other priorities"; "they miss the warning signs"; "they don't think about alternatives"; "they just get sucked in"; "they forget"; "they didn't believe it was important"; "many people have bad habits"; "they didn't think they would get caught"; or "they were just following orders."

But it is seldom easy to elicit these faulty, real-world player behaviors, especially in a way that does not feel like a cheap shot that would undermine the value of the sim.

Given the constraints of our interface, one key designer skill set is hiding the right answer in plain sight. Here are some techniques.

Big Decisions Hidden among Small Decisions

It is natural for players to become overly intellectual in their selection of what to do in a Short Sim. This can be at odds with how they naturally behave.

So, to create straw man around our earlier example, imagine you are taking an Ethics Simulation and are in Part I: All About Ethics. Worst case, the scenario might read something like:

Example of Ethical Challenge:

You are a manager, and you find out your best salesperson is spending more money than he or she is allowed by hospital policy on wining and dining key decision-makers. Do you report this practice to your designated ethical representative or HR liaison?

1. Yes.
2. No.

In contrast, in the real world, we make decisions all of the time, only sometimes with cues on how important they are. One technique then is to present the players with quite a few small, interesting if inconsequential decisions before interjecting the decision that matters.

In the following sim, the player had to ultimately decide if they were going to give the onscreen character some sensitive information or not. To set the player up, I gave them a bunch of short, no-consequence choices they had to make with the onscreen character leading up to the big one.

Here are two examples:

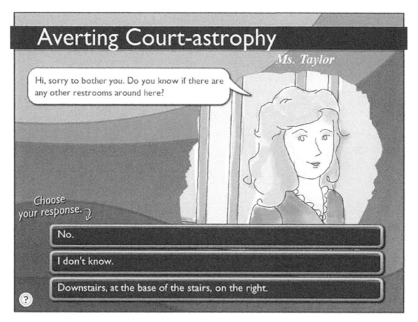

A no-consequence decision positioned the player in the role of a helper. The character will later ask casually for sensitive information.

Note: Any interactions implemented to desensitize users to subsequent big strategic decisions must still be interesting. They can help move the story along, impart key pieces of information, establish personalities and tone, and even help the user define him or herself. They should also be brisk.

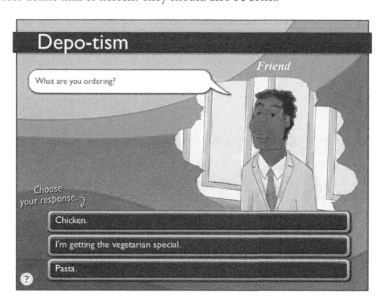

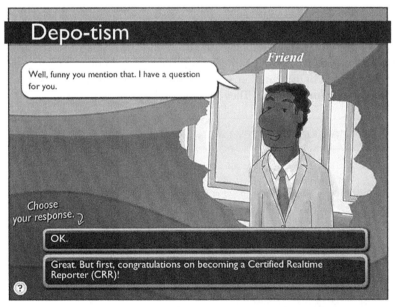

Ten seconds of interactions can set a tone of congeniality, reduce stress around making decision, and convey a bit of background information as well. This interaction happens very early in a short sim, and both encourages the player to act and shows that the actions have some impact.

Unforced Decisions

There are useful techniques around unforced decisions.

Let me back up. Some decisions are *forced*, the equivalent of approaching a "Y" in the road. The player is aware of the decision and is typically more intellectual when choosing a path. But sometimes it is more useful if the sim presents a default path of least resistance, and the mistake is made when players don't interrupt the flow.

The Carpool sim uses the second technique by often allowing players to ask for more options. This technique almost always necessitates training the players early on that asking for additional options, so-called *nested options*, do not always contain the right answer.

This second technique can also be thought of as an example of the power of a consistent interface. If the [More options.] option is often available, the player forgets about it.

We can use other consistent interface schemas to hide in plain sight useful options. Imagine a sim on getting health care workers to wash their hands between patients. We could present a typical day filled with activities (sign in, go to meeting, go to lunch) and present a "Wash Hands" option with every action.

We have also seen in other sims so far a final variation, which is to present a player with a series of completed activities, and for each, we can ask, "Do you see a problem here?" If they do see a problem, we can ask them to identify the problem from a presented list.

Consider Visual Decision-Making to Obscure the Right Answer

Another technique, often used in conjunction with and right after the "Do you see a problem" question, is to obscure the right answer in a multiple choice interface. We saw this "find the problem on this form" minilab sequence in Chapter 7.

The same approach is used here: www.shortsims.com/ch14. See a walkthrough in Appendix 6.

Interrupting Short-Term Success

There is a final variation of the "Unforced Decision" approach. In the real world, wrong decisions are made because of time pressures and the lack of will to stop a smoothly running process. Who wants to stop and maintain the trucks when you are about to get a bonus for most deliveries made in a week?

In the Carpool sim above, there had to be a constant time pressure around some MacGuffin activity for it to evoke a similar feeling. An imminent carpool arriving created that pressure, even in a turn-based static experience. In other sims, there may be an explicit countdown timer of turns left to maximize the discomfort of doing something outside the norm. As in the real world, we can get people to focus on some compelling busywork.

Consider Generic Descriptions to Obscure the Right Answer

Another way to hide a right answer is to use generic and neutral descriptions, rather than direct quotes, for presenting options. Rather than writing:
   "Can you drive me downtown?"

1. Sure. Hop in.
2. I can't. It is against the regulation prohibiting personal rides in staff cars.

One could write instead:
   "Can you drive me downtown?"

1. [Agree and drive her downtown.]
2. [Refuse to drive her downtown.]

Then, on the next screen after the "Refuse" option, you may select a reason, or the coach may fill in with a "You tell her, 'I can't. It is against the regulation prohibiting personal rides in staff cars.'"

Being Influenced by Others

Sims can use strong characters, including manipulative personalities. This makes the experience more interesting, more likely to elicit a faulty behavior from the player, and more realistic.

For example, for an information assurance (cybersecurity) sim used in a secure environment, I wrote:

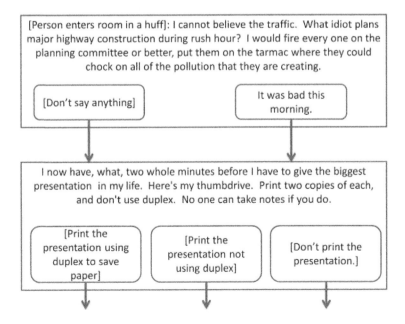

If I have done my job right, the emotional pressure is very high not to choose the right option—[Don't print the presentation] even thought that would involve using a thumb drive which compromises information assurance. Obviously, it was important not to be explicit about the reasons not to print the presentation.

(Alternatively, one can create a highly sympathetic character who is in need of money for example, if the player will have to coach them to turn down work because of a conflict of interest. As in this example, one should not telegraph the real challenge too directly, while still making it realistic. What is efficient is how low-tech the creation of the emotional state can be. It just takes a bit of character building.)

Never Force the Player to Be Immoral or to Make a Mistake They Would Not Make in the Productive World

As we discussed, many learning goals center around someone performing actions they should not do in the real world. I take great pleasure in enticing people to make interesting mistakes. But I never feel right forcing the user into this position.

In the Be a Hacker sim from Chapter 2, there was an option for a player not to steal, even after creating a morally acceptable framework for doing so ("You are stealing from a bad guy").

In one military-sponsored sim on responsible use of personal firearms, the soldiers had to experience what it felt like to fire a weapon either when drunk or when the weather conditions were inclement. We could not simply say, "you had a lot to drink, and now you will be discharging a weapon" as it would be a non-starter for many soldiers. Instead, we created an experiment that put the soldier in a safe laboratory and simulated various impaired conditions for, in the situation of the narrative, doing research. This allowed soldiers to feel the effect of higher blood alcohol or inclement weather conditions when trying to hit a target, while remaining on the moral high ground.

Plenty of content also addresses topics of, "what do you do after you have made a serious mistake." This could be around taking illegal drugs, or cheating on a test, or filling out an expense report inappropriately. Instead of the starting point of the sim being, "You just cheated on a test, and now…," I would start with, "A good friend of yours has come to you for advice. That friend had cheated on a test, and needs your opinion…." This meets the same learning objectives, but without asking the player to do something that he or she would not do.

Here is one partial exception. WILL Interactive did a clever sim on AIDS prevention. In this sim, if the player decided to drink heavily at a party, she lost her ability to later resist sexual advances.

On Conviction Building

Throughout this book, we have explored the opportunities and necessity of building not just *competence* but *conviction*. Conviction, recall, is a strong belief in the importance of something, more enduring and flexible than the closely-related concept of confidence.

Now that we have techniques for getting people to make their real-world mistakes in sims, we can begin to articulate an explicit design pedagogy for accomplishing this.

When *convictions* in players have to be changed or reinforced, levels should be designed with at least some of each of the following:

- Allow the users to experiment with their traditional behavior. Give them the opportunity to do what they would naturally do in a familiar setting. (This is impossible, by the way, in a classroom-based role-play, where people are on their best behavior.)
- When they do something wrong, show them both the immediate, apparent, and high-probability consequences (which are often positive) of their traditional behavior, and the long-term, hidden, and/or "unlikely" but possible consequences (which can be devastating.)
- Visualize the "invisible system," which is the flow of events that people can't normally see, but leads to any problematic outcomes, and described in Chapter 12.
- Allow students to repeat the scenarios (which means they can't be too long or rely too much on linear content), and then "discover" for themselves the right way of doing things. Students can now learn without ever being taught.

For example, in one sim I created on Socratic learning, if a teacher gives the right answer in response to a student question, they receive the praise from the student that they "know everything." But soon the teacher spends all day answering student questions and doesn't have time for more strategic work. A more experienced teacher can instead ask some Socratic questions of the student to encourage the student to answer their own question. The teacher loses the short-term praise but gain more independent and competent students.

The most important design step, of course, is to be honest. Conviction can't be created in a way that does not align with the real world. Famed lawyer Gerry Spence wrote that a critical step in winning an argument is to be on the right side. Similarly, one can only develop convictions in something that is real, if not immediately apparent.

15

Introduction to Advanced Universal Techniques

These next few chapters will discuss fairly advanced techniques in Short Sim design. Many first time designers would be better served by creating a dozen or so simple Short Sims first and then return to this section when done.

However, for those more experienced designers looking to take on more interesting topics and better understand the potential of Short Sims, these advanced techniques will start to scratch that itch. It is worth noting that a few of the techniques in the next few chapters require more advanced authoring environment than just a pure branching engine.

Also, some of the sims I will be presenting starting in Chapter 16 are for audiences aligned with the third level in our tolerance for ambiguity scale in Chapter 5, including college students, soldiers, and high potential employees. While still approachable, the sims require more focus and may best be used with facilitated debriefing, but lead to deeper insights, than previous examples.

Storyboarding and the Language of Cinema

One technique is adding some visual variety to a sim beyond just changing the background. For example, role-plays can involve more cinematic screen layouts. For example:

An establishing shot...

...then shows time passing.

We dolly in…

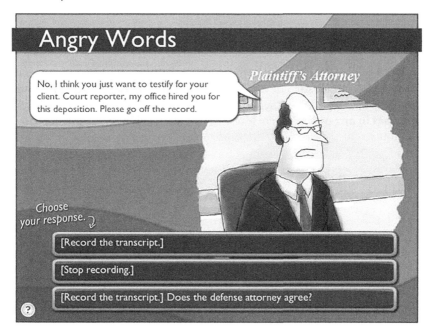

…then pan.

As a reminder, when importing photographs for custom backdrops, consider a slight blur it so as not to distract from the foreground action.

Levels That Can Be Accessed in Any Order

This court reporter ethics sim had a different feature worth mentioning. We discussed the importance of levels in Chapter 12 and focused on presenting levels in a fixed order. In other sims, levels can be accessed individually and sometimes in any order. Where levels can be accessed individually, some may be optional.

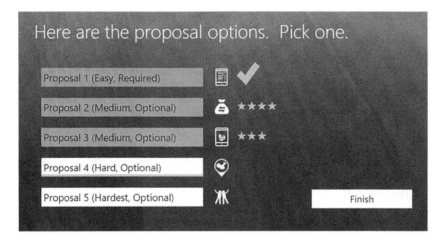

Example of Individually Accessed, But Sequential Levels in a Venture Capitalist Sim

We went even further with the court reporter sims. The client had, through their subject matter interviews, identified fifteen ethical mistakes, from giving personal options on a case to improperly sharing confidential information.

For each of those mistakes, we created a short story-based scenario. (We discussed in Chapter 14 techniques to draw out from users their real-world behaviors.) These become the *levels* in a Short Sim. (We did combine issues where possible.) I then fleshed out the characters and scenarios.

Example of Independent, Individually Accessed Levels

In the final deliverable, the ethics sim presented six random scenarios from the pool of 12. Any player had to get five right to pass.

Easter Eggs

Our final example in this introduction to advanced technique is accessible to anyone and that is the inclusion of Easter eggs. Easter eggs are pieces of interesting content that can be discovered in an experience. One favorite form of Easter egg is different interesting endings to sim, such as shown in the business simulator in Chapter 22. Easter eggs make content more engaging, encourage exploration, put the designer on the same page as the player, and also encourage players to compare experiences.

The inclusion of "Easter eggs" is at odds with the philosophy of creating textbooks or other artifacts of traditional instructional design, which instead feel compelled to explain everything exactly three times, and recoil at the notion that different learners would have different experiences. But the inclusion of a bit of surprise is why games and novels, ironically, often teach better.

Humor, dry and optional, should be thought of as a category of Easter eggs. Clunky humor is worse than no humor of course, but hiding humor provides some cover. And personalities, including both the players' and coaches', are always places to mine. For example,

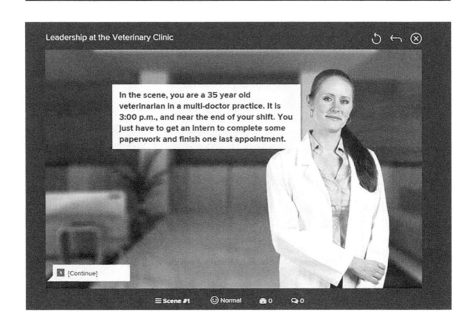

15. Introduction to Advanced Universal Techniques

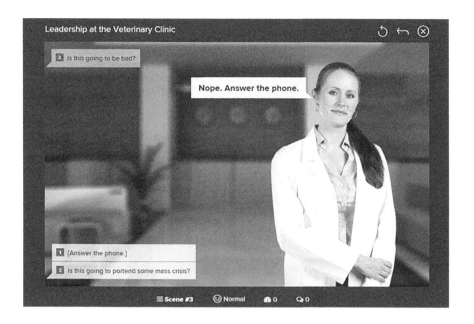

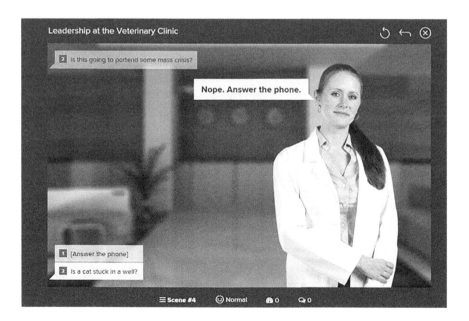

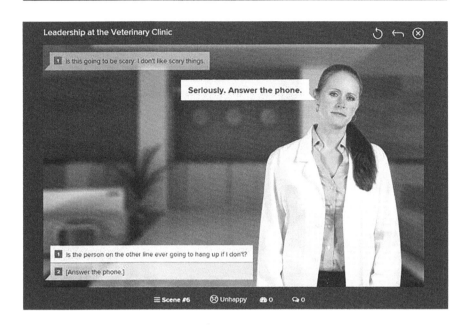

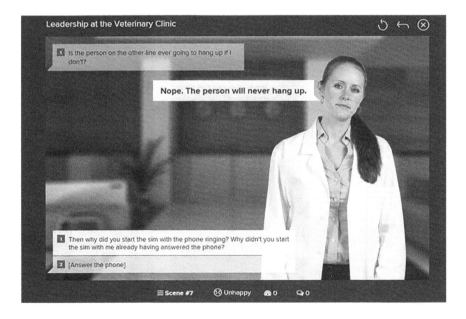

15. Introduction to Advanced Universal Techniques

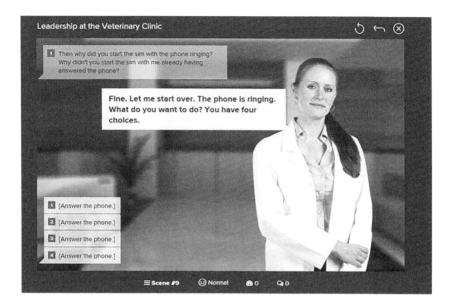

This Easter egg sequence is completely voluntarily. Those who are without humor don't have to engage it or can stop it at any time. But it gives a new user some practice with the interface and sets a tone of knowing comradery.

16

Example

Learning Curves with Complex Topics

Learning curves are easy to understand but nearly limitless in their usefulness and flexibility. Here is a pure, hopefully interesting application of a learning curve. My goal was to help non-math students gain some comfort around looking at scary charts and being able to read them, in this case to support the Econ 101 principle of "areas under the curve."

These sims are for college students who expect a bit more of a challenge than, say, corporate sales people. The content broken up into two parts. Play them to feel yourself climb up a learning curve. You may hit a wall. If you do, sleep on it and try again.

- *Part 1*: Use this link: www.shortsims.com/ch16
  When done, try this.
- *Part 2*: Use this link: www.shortsims.com/ch16

17

Role-Plays, from Simple to Complex

Interpersonal role-plays have been an early, killer app of Short Sims.

Used for everything from leadership and management development to sales and call centers, the role-plays are typically one-on-one conversations that use a basic, branching mechanism.

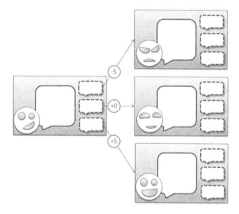

The Mechanics of Basic Branching

To this One-On-One Framework, We Can Easily Make Additions

We have already discussed the addition of a coach, which make Short Sims more engaging and helpful, and even cheaper to develop. A coach introduces a friend, assistant, and mentor to the role-playing genre that had previously almost exclusively used avatars as opponents or barriers to success.

With Multiple Characters

We can also add multiple characters. And one option is to do this easily. The same basic branching mechanics can be used only, as with the inclusion of a coach, with a bit more nuance added to the player options, such as shown in the screenshot below:

The Player and Three Characters

To provide a baseline, here is a sales sim I developed that uses a coach and two characters. (Of note, I did the SME interview on Wednesday, started working on it on Friday, and delivered this version to the client on Monday.) Play it here:

- *Link*: www.shortsims.com/ch17

However, we can be more ambitious still. The opportunity is to create an even more useful interpersonal experience, provided just one more element is added to the mix.

Pushing Further: A Case Study

An organization with a world-wide presence in Information Technology research (let's call them IT Experts, Inc.) wanted to build a suite of complex interpersonal role-play simulations. The goal was to help senior analysts—those who had existing personal and high-trust relationships with Chief Information Officers of large corporations—sell consulting engagements to their clients without risking the privileged relationship and industry objectivity they currently had.

Through a series of interviews with senior analysts all over the world, I learned about the dynamics of their high-stakes client relationships. Here are some notes.

Define Success and Failure

Bad and good outcomes for IT Experts, Inc., in these situations included the following:

- *Failures* include losing the trust of the CIO by overselling; setting up high-value business engagements for competitors by raising issues without positioning their organization as the ones to solve it; and mumbling the sales message and maintaining the status quo relationship (which was the most common current condition).
- *Successes* include agreeing on next steps to explore the topic; being well positioned for a bid; or best of all, walking away with a no-bid contract for IT Experts.

Story Beats

We identified the best microcosm for the role-play as a meeting setup at the client location to share IT Experts, Inc.'s insights about some emerging threat/opportunity to the client's business. The story beats were

- Greeting people at the start of the meeting (starting point, beat zero)
- Starting the conversation/presentation and surfacing big issues (beat one)
- Focusing on understanding and resolving what to do about the problem (beat two)
- Figuring out next steps and roles and responsibilities (beat three)
- Conclusion (end).

Each story beat would consist of four or five interactions. As a result of how the player behaved, the overall situation could get better or worse for the player, succeeding or failing because the player either pushed too hard or did not push hard enough.

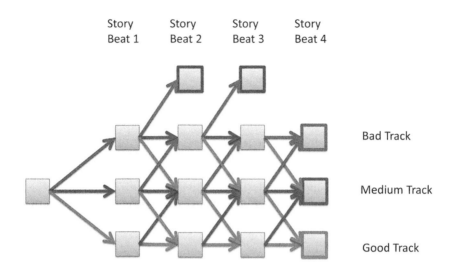

Story Beat 1   Story Beat 2   Story Beat 3   Story Beat 4

Bad Track

Medium Track

Good Track

We then added one more detail.

If we had not, we could have ended up with one of the worst types of interpersonal sims. In bad interpersonal sims:

- Players are presented with streams of dialogue options, but the strategy behind the words is not clear to the player when making them.
- Feedback feels arbitrary and unfair. That situation can quickly devolve to where the player starts making random choices.
- Players often can neither articulate what they learned nor apply it.

The Theory of the Case

At this point, we identified the "theory of the case." This would simplify and organize the experience.

We realized that the client's awareness could grow, from:

- Starting with a low understanding of the disruptive technology problem and need for action to building a high understanding, and/or
- Starting with a low desire to involve IT Experts in the implementation of the solution to building a high desire.

I paired these two goals into a single, two-dimensional, consultant-style graph.

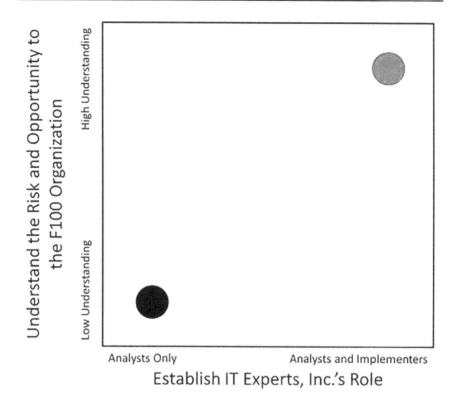

Establish IT Experts, Inc.'s Role

The player would start the meeting with a client who neither understood the technology problem (such as cybersecurity, new fabrication approaches, or cloud computing) nor believed the player could help with the implementation. This position was in the bottom left, represented by the black circle's current position.

The goal was to teach the client about the problem and establish IT Expert's experience in fixing it (move the black ball to the upper right, represented by the gray circle.)

The player had two productive activities in the meeting to "move the ball":

- They could *teach* their clients and help them understand the need for action.
- They could *convince* their clients that they could do the implementation work.

For example,

- The player could ask his or her colleague, a subject expert from IT Expert Inc., to chime in on a topic ("what are typical cyber security vulnerabilities with tablet computers?"), which would move the black ball straight up.

- Or the player could mention work they had done for other large organizations ("We did a similar project with General Motors last quarter, and improved their…"), which would move the ball to the right.

We decided to visualize this map in the bottom right of the sim's screen. The black ball would move with every statement, by both the player and other people in the room. We used a consistent four decision interface (nudge the ball up, down, left, or right) across all of the player actions.

A time element was then added to the sim design. Meeting participants would lose interest if this journey took too many turns.

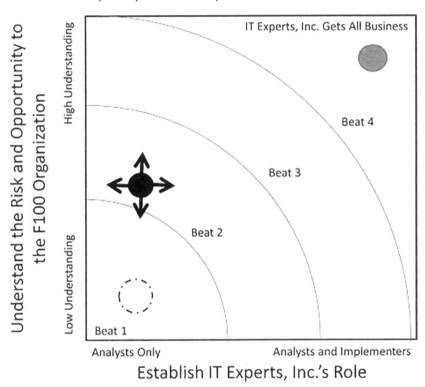

Establish IT Experts, Inc.'s Role

Finally, we identified the best practices path. More specifically, we identified the inverse: the paths that led players to failure in the real world.

- If the player started the meeting pushing too hard on the implementation successes of IT Experts, Inc. (going to quickly to the right), the meeting would end with an unhappy F100 client, thinking IT Experts as just another vendor looking out for themselves.
- If the player simply gave the client all of the information and perspective they needed without any positioning of their consultants (in other

17. Role-Plays, from Simple to Complex

words, moving the ball too quickly straight up), they would end the meeting with no new business but their reputation intact (which was the most common, real-world occurrence.)

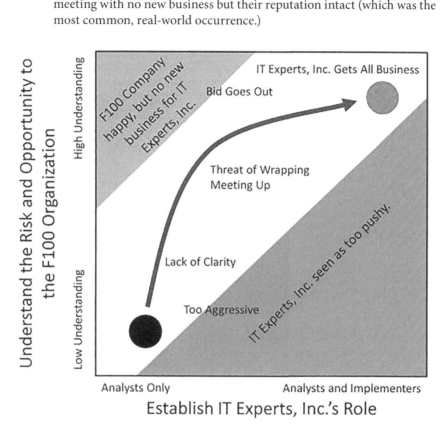

Establish IT Experts, Inc.'s Role

Across the beats, it became clear to players through a few repeat plays that the safest course was to traverse the chart in a slight bow, erring initially on the side of helping the CIO understand the situation, but then breaking to the right before the meeting could be called.

- If, for example, the black ball was moving up too quickly and not enough to the right, perhaps driven by one of the characters in the room, the player could tap on the breaks by introducing another element to complicate the topic ("But the situation gets harder when two factor authentication is introduced…."), pushing the black ball down out of the red.

From a design perspective, we could focus our development resources in the above white space and end the sim quickly when the room drifted out.

This "theory of the case" helped us as designers focus on the meaningful interactions. It also eventually allowed for the players to try a variety of strategies, such as seeing how aggressively and quickly they could push the consulting business without getting burned. The experience felt fair, and it felt transferable. From this solid framework, a slew of flourishes and variations were possible.

Rigorous Design

Figuring out this graphic was challenging. It is not necessary for many role-play Short Sims. But for this high-stakes sim, it was time well worth spending. The worst part of a branching interface is that it can allow designers to get sloppy. This "Theory of the Case" graphic forced a rigor. And eventually, the graphic worked its way into other training material.

18

Example

Openish-Ended Labs Around Supply and Demand

With Short Sims, one can build cheap, reusable, infinitely scalable labs of all sorts. Any of the methodologies in this book can be used to create labs. The first sim of this book, Be a Hacker, is more lab than anything else.

But the following approach allows the most direct creation of a simple, but still open-ended, experience that both teaches and tests knowledge. This approach can model the behaviors of pieces of equipment, computer programs, and even chemical interactions.

To understand this approach, consider a scenario. You are making your own cranberry sauce. You have to combine some amount of water, sugar, and whole cranberries, and then bring the mixture to a boil before chilling. After some number of experiments and taste tests, you can get the exact proportions right. (Or you give up and buy the canned stuff like everyone else.)

From a Short Sim designer perspective, that situation is only slightly more complex than the Demand Curve Sim described in Chapter 13, which also allowed for the tweaking of a few variables and observing the reaction.

Realistically, every additional "dial" we add to the mix significantly increases complexity of use and creation. One of the Short Sims I created probably went as far as most people will ever want to go in creating an open-ended(ish) lab using this method. It was also used in the same college level series around the intersection of demand and supply curves. It assumed an audience that valued rigor in content.

Play it for yourself here:

- *Link*: www.shortsims.com/ch18

The core game-play presents a situation with four switches and gives the player the ability to keep flipping them back and forth. (One switch had four possible states, one with three states, and two with two.) Math people will have already figured out that 4 * 2 * 3 * 2 means that there are forty eight states I had to assemble.

I tend to organize the states into a grid to make wiring easier.

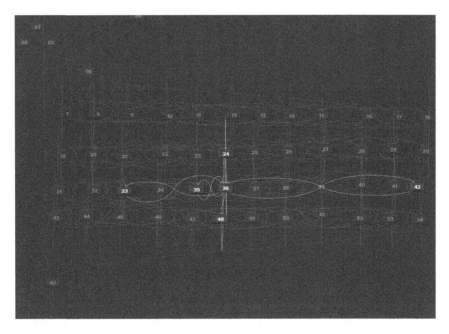

Under the covers in an open-ended Lab with four levers and a single victory condition.

A consistent user interface is almost always necessary to make the experience engaging. The section that sets up the lab is considerably less interactive:

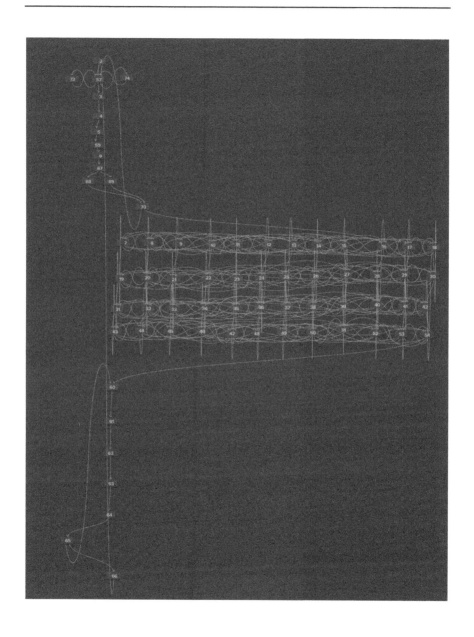

Here is how the sim begins:

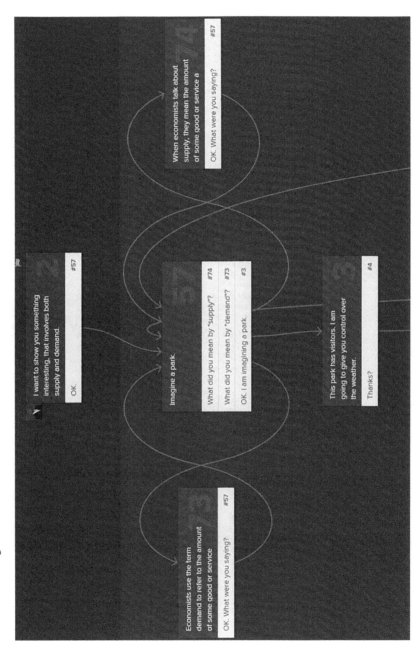

18. Openish-Ended Labs Around Supply and Demand

And this is how the brief knowledge test is structured (with graphics):

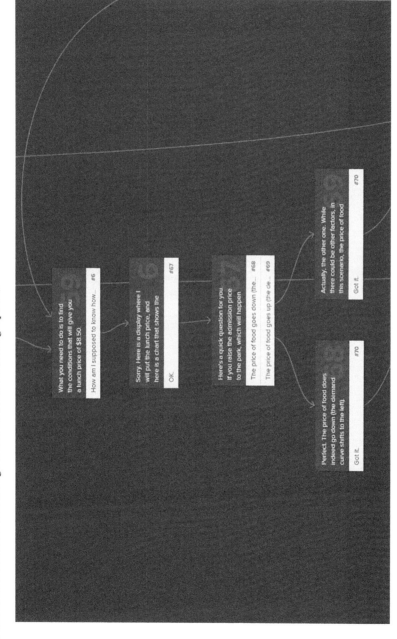

A Wide Range

Short Sims are well structured to present labs. They can cover almost anything, from technical equipment, or broader social concepts. They can be highly chaperoned or can allow motivated learners to flip switches on and off, as in this case, or otherwise explore to see what happens. And lab interactions, big or minilabs may be the best way to verify that users are paying attention in any Short Sim type.

19

Examples of Sandboxes and Other Exploration of Interesting Systems

Academics have a long history of producing systems diagrams. These are often abstracted models showing the interconnections between different parts.

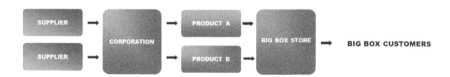

One System Model: A Supply Chain

No matter how accurate, these charts can come off as static, even smug. There are no emotions or stakes. There is no agency: The creation, maintenance, adaption, or disruption challenges are all swept under the rug.

Still, these diagrams are useful and often form the basis for *learning objectives* for a course or chapter.

Consider three examples of systems that students or employee taking various courses may have to understand:

1. "Credit cards have to attract two different sides of a market: the consumers and the merchants. Behaviors that advantage one side may cause abandonment by the other, ultimately hurting both sides."
2. "Companies are part of an ecosystem of suppliers and customers, with both aligning and competing goals."
3. "Marketing plans for businesses should consider Four P's: Product, Place, Price, and Promotions."

Short Sims can be used to develop a deeper knowledge and greater conviction for all three.

Of course, any of these systems can be presented using the simple, process-centric Short Sims of earlier chapters. However, if the audience is more thoughtful and strategic, a more exploratory and open-ended approach may be warranted.

As we said in Chapter 7, an early challenge for any designer is to decide, for the sim, "who is doing the doing." We must identify a person in a role who is trying to achieve some goal in the context of the system. Then, we need to flesh out the situation to create the microcosm. As always, the less explaining that has to be done, the better.

Here are three examples of exploratory Short Sims, which are executions of teaching each of the systems mentioned above. The next chapter provides a deeper dive into a fourth example.

Example One: Two-Sided Markets

For a suite of sims, one learning objective was to develop an awareness of two-sided markets and the challenges of making both sides happy. Specifically, in the credit card industry, credit card companies have to meet the needs of both the merchants and consumers in order to grow. As with so many concepts, the goal was not just to raise awareness but to actually build conviction.

So in this sim, users have to balance the needs of two groups while also growing the overall market size.

This slide introduces the challenge. And importantly, the scale image on the right will be the visual metaphor throughout.

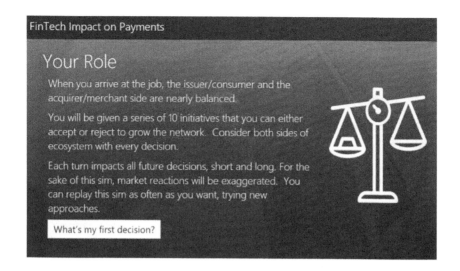

The gameplay is simple. Each turn, the user, as ombudsman for the company's ecosystem, makes a binary choice to either accept or reject a specific proposal which has implications to both sides, consumers and merchants. As a pedagogical bonus, the player also learns about the industry issues and initiatives through the nature of the questions. (I added arrows on these screenshots to show what choices were made.)

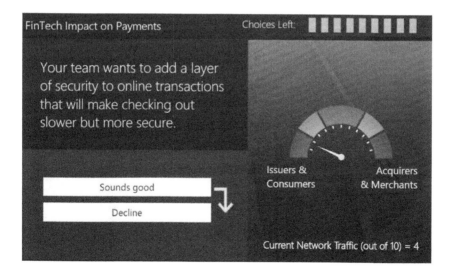

A dial that echoes the scale is shown on each screen, showing to which side the market was currently tipping. I also included a countdown timer of number of choices still to be made through yellow bars in the upper right of the screen.

Every user action produces a "Results" screen that shows the extrinsic implications of the decision.

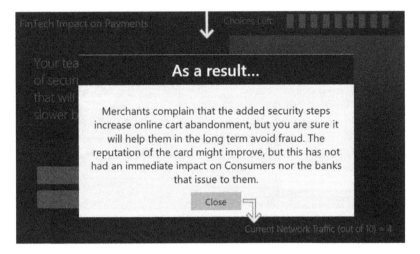

As in life, the player has two goals: Maintain the balance and grow the network, which sometimes are at odds in the short term.

This sim presents ten binary choices. (I happen to love interesting binary decisions, which become powerful over many turns.) We stuck with ten decisions, even though generically seven choices is a better target number for most sims. We mapped out ten, planning to edit out the weakest three, but just happened to like all of the issues.

If the player favors one side over the other too significantly, the market destabilizes, causing one side to collapse and taking the whole network down.

In the event of failure, the feedback also explains which sides began the collapse.

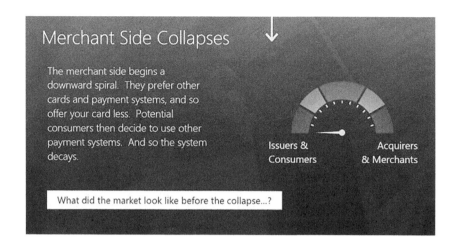

Note: Choices are cumulative. Mathematical calculations were maintained to track the aggregated impact of the decisions of each player for each game. This sim used both long- and short-term variables.

Below is the calculations performed for an activity that in the short term helps merchants (and acquirers) and hurts issuers (and consumers), but also has a long-term negative impact on both sides.

☐ Accept 1

Add <u>2.00</u> to Acquirer
   When the user clicks

Subtract <u>2.00</u> from Issuer
   When the user clicks

Subtract <u>0.25</u> from Issuer_Long_Term
   When the user clicks

Subtract <u>0.25</u> from Acquirer_Long_Term
   When the user clicks

Show layer <u>Feedback-Accept</u>
   When the user clicks

Most users replayed the sim two to three times. In about ten minutes, they gained comfort with and conviction around the material and understand how important the issue was for the entire company.

Example Two: The Distribution Sim

I had to create a sim that presented distribution models to college students, trying to get them to see beyond the boxes to the real companies and challenges that connect them.

Here is what I created:

- *Link*: www.shortsims.com/ch19

The user has a goal of getting a good valuation from an investor, which was just a proxy for "good business results," but also gave me a way of ending the sim prematurely if the player gets on a bad track.

At its core, this sim took a sandbox approach. It exists just to mess around. There are plenty of ways of playing to get very different results. But as long as the user plays through few times, regardless of the results, he or she will experience channel conflict, disintermediation, and other issues that are more interesting to users when *their* actions create the problems.

Some other design notes are as follows:

- The user *options* are consistent between turns.
- The graphics evolve from more literal to more abstract. The dashboard forces awareness of the various constituents.
- The graphics were assembled in PowerPoint from clip art and simple shapes.
- There are also many endings, so users can compare how they ended up. Different endings, including some very obscure ones, can increase "buzz" between users as they compare results.
- The outside investor construct avoids any slow death scenario by quickly pulling the plug after a few bad decisions.

It is easy to see how this Short Sim could be made with much higher production values down the road.

Example Three: The Four P's of Marketing

The final of the three sims helps the students understand the Four P's of Marketing.

- *Link*: www.shortsims.com/ch19

Some design notes are as follows:

- Yes, there is a shark's dorsal fin in the water.

- The colors are used consistently. Green tints are used for options. Orange tints are new building opportunities. Red is used for competitors. Black-and-white buildings are not currently impactful. Full-color buildings are structures influenced by the player.
- The two-dimensional people show popularity.
- The "retire" date adds a countdown timer.
- Players can evolve their one store operation in many different directions. There are eight endings, a mix of successful and unsuccessful. Depending on how the Four P's are played, success can be creating generic ice cream as a no-name producer or a super-premium ice cream boutique. Below is the architecture for the sim, roughly going from top to bottom.

The architecture of the sim looked like this:

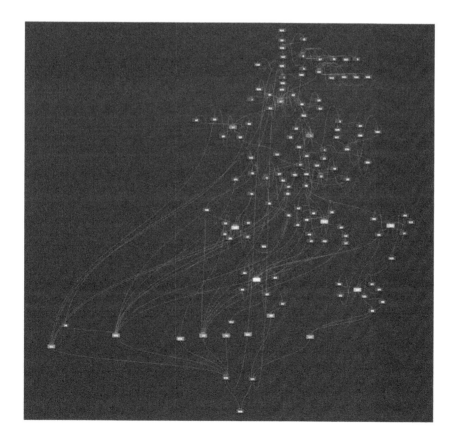

Background History: My Personal Journey to Short Sims

These sandboxes come closer to producing Short Sims that feel more like computer games. This is not a coincidence. Short Sims have their origin in full educational simulations. Here is why, starting two decades ago.

I was the research analyst who launched Gartner's eLearning coverage. I wrote in a 1999 Gartner Research Note that "Lessons learned from the computer games industry will increasingly impact the evolution of corporate e-learning."[1] In my column for Online Learning magazine a few months later, I wrote "Probably the best model to fill the hole [in sophisticated content] will be immersive simulations — courses that put students into a role and give them a problem to solve." And in my 2002, "Field Guide to Educational Simulations," for Learning Circuits, I started again with the question, "Can the lessons, techniques, and technologies of computer games be intelligently applied to create a new breed of formal learning simulations?"[2] while simultaneously cautioning, "Simulations are sparking excitement in the e-learning world. And yet, simulations—especially soft skill simulations—are approaching the peak of inflated expectations. Everyone's talking about simulations, but few have seen a model they like."

The early premise—that computer game-like simulations would be highly appropriate for education—is intuitive. Certainly linear content was deadening. And computer games were, after all, complex teaching machines, combining scalability and conviction building better than any other educational experience to date. Students could play thirty to sixty hours of the newest version of *Civilization*, an oft-cited example, and be excited and interested in the topic. Players could experience the pros and cons of starting wars, investing in technology, and expanding national influence through culture and religion.

However, while the idea of computer game-inspired educational media was perfect in theory, in too often broke down in practice. Creating a fun game—forget even making it educational—is very hard. Meanwhile, the number of hours that went into the development of Civilization was astronomical, when all the versions, and all of the user communities, are taken into account. This reduced its use as a role model; there are no patrons willing to invest that much over that long of a period. Finally, for today's environment, it is the wrong solution; most academic, military, or corporate courses do not need or want a deep, thirty- to sixty-hour educational experience that fully engages 30% of the audience. They want a broad collection of ten- or fifteen-minute programs that engage 85% or more of the audience. This may have been why, for a decade and a half, no game-like educational sim became a killer app, the equivalent of the VisiCalc spreadsheet for the Apple II series.

---

[1] Aldrich, C. E-Learning Lessons from the Computer Games Market: Three New Rules—Seen Today in Practices of Leading Game Manufacturers and Their Consumers—Will Differentiate E-learning From Traditional Training. Gartner Research Note COM-09-7081, December 13, 1999.

[2] Aldrich, C. *Field Guide to Educational Simulations*, Learning Circuits: American Society for Training and Development, 2002.

But I am jumping ahead.

Starting at the beginning of this millennium, I started building some very complex educational simulations for a broader population, which were patent and award winning, and made millions. On my most popular, SimuLearn's Virtual Leader, I studied plays and implementations carefully over years. I noticed that many stakeholders—students, instructors, sponsors, and those using simulations for assessment—that considered the rich accuracy of the experience initially a positive, began seeing it as a negative. It was too open-ended. The lessons learned were not obvious or exaggerated enough. Across tens of thousands of plays, the best case happened when student fell into one of five or six predictable strategies in the game, which lined up with various leadership styles, and then had a debriefing session with a coach to talk through it. (Virtual Leader was also very hard to show during a conference presentation—it was too subtle and nuanced. In fact, all computer games are very hard to show unedited for a minute or two to a broad audience.)

During this time, I had another role. As well as developing complex sims (the rules of which I put in my 2009 book, *The Complete Guide to Simulations and Serious Games*[3]), I was often in the sales situation of pitching new sim concepts to corporations and government agencies. These were, as you can imagine, rather high-stakes presentations.

For each, I would spend some time studying the material, and then would I build out robust storyboards, typically in PowerPoint, of the sim I imagined.

The first ten or fifteen slides took the audience through the first, easy level of the proposed sim. It showed a few moments where players could make right or wrong decisions, and the feedback for each. They learned the interface.

At the end of this first level, someone in the meeting room would predictably say, "Yes, that is interesting, but it seems too simple." That would be my cue to go to my second set of storyboards that jumped ahead in the proposal to a sequence of the gameplay about mid-sim. These five or six slides, more high level than moment to moment, would visualize a more complex situation with the application of deeper strategy and nuanced actions.

Finally, I might end with three or four slides of other possible levels, and the challenges they present. These mid and end sim storyboards were effective because the people in the room had joined me in going through the first level.

At this point, if I had done my job, the people in the room would be itching to play the proposed sim. They would even be talking about different approaches they might use in the more challenging scenarios I had teed up.

I won some of these contracts and lost others. Typically, the reason I lost was cost and time to build, in many cases despite the need for the value I was proposing and the interest of the sponsors. Interestingly, when I did win the contracts, often enough, the final, complex sims were only really effective for a third of the audience, mixed for a third, and not appealing at all to the last third.

---

[3] Aldrich, Clark. *The Complete Guide to Simulations and Serious Games: How the Most Valuable Content Will Be Created in the Age beyond Gutenberg to Google.* San Francisco: Pfeiffer, 2009.

Then, around the middle of this decade, some important non-profits began asking me for smaller sims to support some incredibly important work, including for assessment. Soon after, some tool vendors started producing authoring tools that were created explicitly for making branching stories, but also flexible enough to do much more. And I was increasingly getting involved in conversations with content designers who had read my books and believed in what I was saying, but did not have access to the various exotic skills and budgets necessary to pull off big sims.

The conflation of these experiences led me down an almost five year journey. During this time, I created hundreds of Short Sims for clients. My research question was simply, what is the current intersection between meaningful interactivity and broad stakeholder comfort in educational media? This book contains the successful resolution of that most interesting question.

That is why the best way to describe some of the best of Short Sims is "a sim of a sim." Given my experiences, I can think of no higher goal.

On Rigor

A sim of a sim is a powerful approach. But the Short Sim methodology is highly susceptible to sloppy design that frustrates any illusion.

As often as possible for sandbox sims, I figure out how a dynamic computer game would crunch variables, and then "prerender" that math into the branching structures. Spreadsheets can be useful for this.

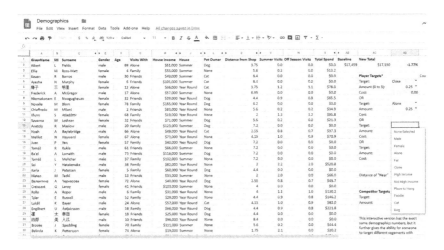

A Short Sim implementation may be state-based, but the underlying calculations, such as in this case, can be rigorous.

20

Endings

In the design of any Short Sim, it is critical to stick the landing. Endings—successes, failures, or mixed—should include combinations of the following elements.

What Happens Next

The sim ought present what happens next as a result of player actions. Many of the more interesting Short Sims I designed have seven or eight failure narratives and three or four successes.

In a leadership simulation, for example, a failure ending may present, "Even though your staff agreed with your ideas in the meeting, no one put much effort into executing them and two key people asked to be transferred to different divisions." This plays to the strengths of a Short Sim, showing players the consequences of their actions they may not see in the real world, by either speeding up time, increasing bad luck, or showing consequences out of sight. If done perfectly, both the short-term positive feedback (people agreeing in the meeting) and the long-term negative (but nothing happened) would line up with the player's real-world experiences if they had gone through a similar situation.

In good sims, the ending narratives provide the under-appreciated information of "what success looks like," and "what failure looks like."

Explicit Lessons Learned

Endings can also include summaries of learning objectives. This ending not only contains the exact rules that needed to be followed, but also why they are important.

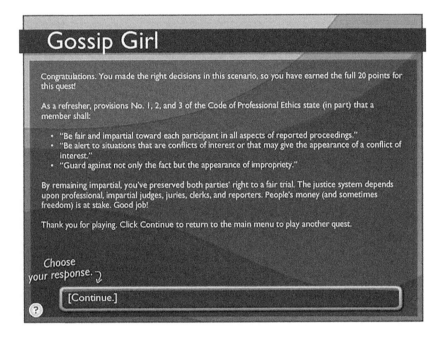

A concluding screen restating learning points and impact

Scores and Stars

Short Sims can present both:

- Open-ended scores
- Bounded stars (or some other relative framework, such as letter grades).

The *open-ended score* allows for competition, while the *stars* allow players to answer the question, "But how did I do?"

Done well, the combination can lead to increased Short Sim replay. Zero stars may require a user to try again if credit is somehow being issued, and one star may be a low pass. Some players will be satisfied with less than perfect scores, while others may shoot for the highest possible.

While just one is fine, the combination of scores and stars provide an open-ended and nuanced result with a simple framework that allow players to understand how well they did.

And a Chance to Try Again

With the possible exception of assessment programs, all Short Sims should provide the opportunity for players to play again or not.

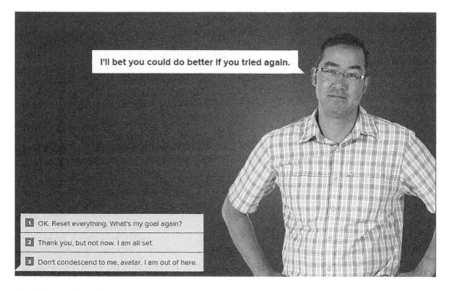

Start the entire sim over

Not all Failures Should Require Restarting the Entire Sim

What should happen when a player makes a critical mistake?

Not all failures should force the sim to end. In fact, quite a few don't. In sims developing comfort in linear processes, a player mistake may simply get a short notice, with the chance to make the specific decision over again. Players then do a variation of "rewind" and try again. In these sims, mini-failures may always be just one click away. (These failures screens should still explain why the mistake was made, and perhaps some brief, negative consequences had it happened.)

In broader, more complex systems-based sims, explicit failures may require restarting the entire experience. With this higher-stakes approach, failures often should require multiple bad moves, or one extra bad move.

A Good Taste

When creating the ending of the sim, whether after a successful or unsuccessful play, I often think of how a maître d'hotel should act towards a customer exiting the restaurant. The sim should not waste the time of the player, but any coach should be grateful and respectful and provide a final taste to encourage a return visit.

21

Assessments and Measuring Learning and Engagement

Some designers will need to create Short Sims for formal assessment. And all Short Sims can be tracked to provide better insight into learning and engagement than traditional media. Let's start with formal assessment.

Assessment Short Sims

Short Sims are ideal for formal assessments. They can be used for everything from evaluating competence with processes, to completing multi-stage equations, to testing mindsets and biases. They can be used for candidate pre-screening, certification, emergency readiness, and summative standardized tests.

To set the stage, assessment Short Sims follow the default approach described in this book of a collection of decision-filled first-person levels and scenarios.

For example, suppose an organization had the goal of assessing health care workers' knowledge of when to wash their hands during the course of a day. The assessment Short Sim might put the player in the role of a nurse or doctor going various places in a hospital and doing such activities as seeing a handful of patients, going to a staff meeting with a sick co-worker, having lunch, and being pulled into an emergency situation, all with ubiquitous options of washing hands.

Most of the time, the process of creating assessment Short Sims will predictably have both similarities to and differences from the processes discussed so far in this book.

How Assessment Short Sims Are Similar to Educational Short Sims

The process of creating a Shot Sim to *assess* competence and conviction is very similar to that of creating a Short Sim to *develop* competence and conviction.

Learning/Assessment Objectives

As with creating any Short Sim, the necessary first step is to identify, to varying degrees of specificity, what the learning/assessment objectives are.

Research

The research process includes interviewing experts about common mistakes and varying approaches to problems. Again, the two lines of questing are, "What are the two or three right ways of doing this?" and "What mistakes do people make, and why?" At the end of the process, it is reasonable to assume you will have the material for ten to fifteen assessment items (moments of truths).

Situation

The designer has to create an environment where such competence and conviction are needed or otherwise demonstrated. They situation answers the question, "Who is doing what, and why?" In some cases, the environment can be purely abstract, such as around mathematics.

Stories and Levels

A designer then has to figure out the stories and the levels of which they are comprised. Typically, a *level* will cover at least two assessment items. Then, a good rule is to use as few different *stories* as possible. (A Short Sim switches stories when it changes the character that the player is playing, or the time and place that the character occupies. Shifts can be disorienting, increase the *cognitive load* of the player, and take up time non-productively with the learning objectives. Every time an assessment switches stories, it increases assessment fatigue.)

In our hand-washing assessment example, we can likely do most or all of the content is one cohesive story. This is made easier by the fact that making wrong choices, such as over-washing hands, not washing hands, or washing the wrong way, has no immediate, narrative stopping consequences.

Decisions

The look and feel, and the creation itself, of the decisions and decision options are identical. There may be a slightly higher threshold to get the wording exactly right and a slightly lower tolerance for more abstract or edge case situations.

How Assessment Short Sims Are Different than Educational Short Sims

There are, of course, a few critical differences in the design approach.

Planning Questions

Questions that impact strategy have to be answered in assessment Short Sims that are not part of the planning for developmental Short Sims. These include:

1. Is the assessment timed?
2. Can players go back and change answers in a simulation? When are such options available? (This puts further pressure to minimize feedback.)
3. Is there a risk of cheating? Could answers be published online somewhere? (This may require the construction of multiple versions.)
4. What happens if someone fails the test? Do they retake the same test, or a different test, or just fail, or something else?

Scoring Mechanism

An assessment program keeps track of the right or wrong decisions, and stores them in centralized repositories often through a cloud database or a learning management system. Authoring environments typically have the ability to capture and transmit scores based on the player's actions.

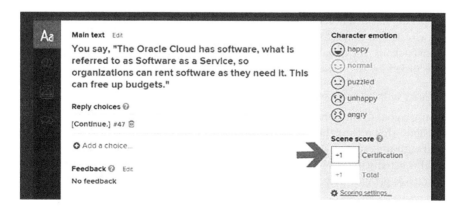

Some authoring environments allow designers to impact score by *scene (aka slide or node)*, and others allow scores to changes by the logically identical *link chosen*.

Scoring can be like darts, where a higher score is better, or it can be like golf, where the player may try to accomplish something in as few turns as possible. In most assessment implementations, the designer will simply put a score of one with every right choice.

Lack of Feedback/Lack of Ability of Start Over or Replay Segment

The sine qua non of a *developmental Short Sim* is providing feedback and often retries. In fact, the core mechanics of developmental Short Sims that we presented earlier is based on feedback and retires.

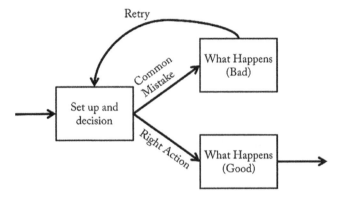

The core mechanic of developmental Short Sims

However, *assessment Short Sims* should, most of the time, offer significantly less feedback with regards to how right or how wrong a decision was and fewer retries to a player than developmental Short Sims.

(There can be exceptions. When the golf-approach to scoring is used, such as if a person has to solve some math problems or use some tool in the fewest steps, the assessment may show them what happens when they will hit a wall, and let them back up. The penalty for such mistakes is increased number of turns, which is recorded.)

Rolling with Punches

Again, a goal in the construction of Short Sims is to use as few distinct stories as possible. This means that Short Sims designers often have to figure out a way to "roll with the punches" of player wrong decisions.

This usually involves a more aggressive use of *diverting* the narrative. Diverted narratives provide players with parallel paths, with similar story beats that may be written differently and with different possible available decisions. While these are used extensively in developmental Short Sims to provide feedback, agency, and narrative variety, they are used almost exclusively in simple assessments to avoid tipping off a player to the rightness or wrongness of a decision.

The structure of diverging and then integrating narrative can look like this:

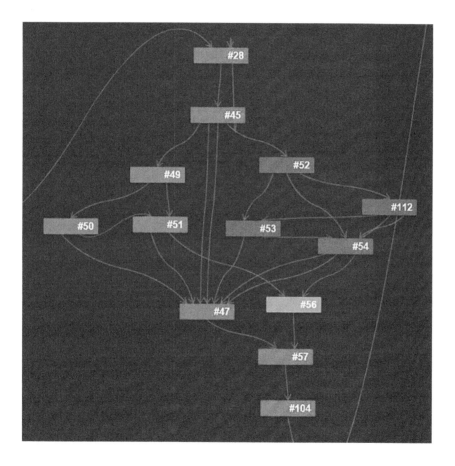

The choices made in #45 can take players down different paths, including the #49 and #52 paths. The narrative re-integrates at #57.

In our hand-washing assessment, a diversion may occur when a hand-washing station is broken. The player may seek out a new station, use latex gloves instead, report the broken station, or just directly approach the patient. In any of the options, the students will, after a unique story beat or two, continue to see the patient, at which point the various story paths quickly re-integrates.

For another example, if a player was applying a series of mathematical processes to an equation, the diversion may continue playing out an early, wrong calculation.

Consider a two part, simple question:

- A field is in the shape of a rectangle, 50 feet by 200 feet.
- Part A. How many feet of fencing is needed to fence the perimeter?
- Part B. If the cheap fencing cost $17 a foot, how much would it cost to fence the perimeter?

The responsive (i.e., roll with the punches) approach may be to first, ask the Part A question:

Part A. How many feet of fencing is needed to fence the perimeter?

A. 250
B. 500
C. 750
D. 10,000

Then, based on the answer of Part A, customize Part B.

Part B. If fencing cost $17 per foot, how much will it cost to fence in the field, based on your Part A answer of 750?

A. $5,250
B. $6,000
C. $8,025
D. $12,750

This approach also allows for a partial credit system. The alternative is to create two situations.

Part A: A field is in the shape of a rectangle, 50 feet by 200 feet.
How many feet of fencing is needed to fence the perimeter?
Part B: A second field has the perimeter of 1,120 feet.
If fencing cost $17 per foot, how much will it cost to fence that field?

Here is another, more visual example:

Parallelogram **ABCD** is shown in the coordinate plane.

Part A) Which of the following shapes represents ABCD after a rotation of 180° about the origin?

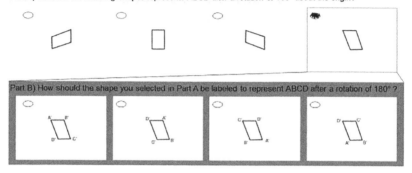

Here, a student has to answer two parts to a question, with the second part's options dependent on the answer selected in the first part. (Note, at this point, the student has already answered the first part incorrectly.)

The Introduction

One other change, of course, is in the introduction text. For example:

This is part of the final test.

You will be presented with a series of decisions. Make you choices in accordance with the material you have learned.

You cannot go back or retake any part of this, so choose carefully. Your results here will impact your eligibility for certification.

Assessments Are a Perfect Use of Short Sims

That assessment is a perfect use of Short Sims is not a coincidence. To reiterate from Chapter 3, The Short Sim philosophy was honed with assessment being a key requirement.

- They provide a methodology for presenting multiple stage problems, including partial credit.
- They arc 508 compliant.
- They are very simple to use compared with other interactive content, but still allow for a wide range of experiences.
- Short Sims produce a relatively small number of discrete outcomes (perhaps five to ten) versus the nearly infinite outcomes of more dynamic models.

- They evolve from, and are compatible with, the item-creation culture of current assessment processes. An assessment company can transition current item-authors to Short Sims. The costs are aligned. They can even coexist with traditional items on the same electronic page.
- There is no randomness, so they are always auditable and fair.
- They allow for, but do not require, a transition into more valuable areas such as interpersonal dynamics, visual problem solving, short feedback loops, and next-generation skills such as leadership and adaptiveness.
- They reduce test fatigue.

Measuring Learning and Learner Engagement

Dedicated assessment sections, however, are only an optional part of broader strategies for measuring learning and learner engagement. Let's zoom out.

To understand and calibrate any use of Short Sims, many organizations want to use metrics to answer two sets of questions:

- *Learner Performance*: How well does the course improve learners? Are there important points that large numbers of learners are not getting?
- *Learner Engagement*: When and why do learners disengage from the content, either physically or emotionally?

Learners' Performance

The most important issue is *learner performance*, even in programs that don't have dedicated assessment sections. Here are tactics that leading organizations are using.

Measuring Moments of Truth

Organizations start by identifying and tracking how learners do in *critical decisions* near the end of the course. Are 70% of learners making the right decisions? If not, the course has to be rebuilt to better reinforce these concepts. Alternatively, if 95% of the learners are getting them right, it may be useful to make these *moments of truth* a bit more challenging. This approach obviously includes an assessment section if one is used, but it neither requires one nor is it restricted to one.

Measuring Habits

A second layer is to identify and track how learners adopt target habits across the course. Depending on the course, these could be around "customer service," "ecosystem thinking," "focus on profitability," "security and fraud protection," or "adherence to policies" in a corporate setting; or "application of the scientific process," "fighting confirmation bias," "the Socratic Method," or "showing work," in academics.

We identify every relevant decision across all of the sims in the course per each target habit, and then track learner activities separately. We record a +1 for every time a learner makes the right choice, and a −1 for every time a learner makes a wrong choice.

From this approach, we see patterns. Every learner should be getting more of these as they progress in the course, even as the decisions get harder and more nuanced.

Patterns and conclusions:

Target Habits (such as fraud control) Across Course

Total Score of Early 10 Sim Decisions	Total Score of Last 10 Sim Decisions	Conclusion
Low	High	The course seems to be working.
High	High	The learner already has the habit, but it is being reinforced.
Low	Low	The course is not improving habits.
High	Low	The course is developing the wrong habits.

Factor in Confidence and Conviction Levels

Some organizations go deeper than this. We can also look at the *time* it takes for learners to make decisions. Right answer made with low conviction (takes more than six seconds) can serve as a 50% proxy for wrong answers for the purposes of analysis.

For example, consider the questions:

What is 3!

a. 6
b. 9
c. 27

Or

A person applying for a passport is using a photograph that is nine months old, and her hair is a different color and cut. Do you, as the agent,

E. Accept the photograph?
F. Tell the applicant that the photograph will not be accepted?

If we are taking into account confidence/conviction levels, learners who get the right answer but take more than six seconds do not get a +1 score, but −0.5.

Factor in Demographic Information

To better understand the results, we can then also factor in personnel information in any regression analyses. Specifically:

- Are right and wrong answers geographically correlated?
- Are right and wrong answers correlated around job experience (grade)?
- Are right and wrong answers correlated around role or background?

When correlations are found, there may be one of two root causes. The first is that our program is getting caught up by some sweeping organizational issues (morale crisis in Arizona), or second, the program has biases that exclude certain segments.

The go-ahead plan for the second possibility is language and content reviews by people from that demographic, with the possibility of a forked version being developed and launched for that community.

Factor in Real-World Data

The Shorts Sims can also be measured against real-world data where that is available. Specifically, we can compare:

- The performance of learners compared to their course experiences to identify where the course failed to develop the necessary skills.
- The performance of learners who went through the course compared to those that did not.
- The performance of learners and their assessment scores to validate accurate.

Engagement

After learner performance, the other important set of questions is around learner engagement.

We start here by looking at course *dropouts*. This is something that organizations want to reduce directly, but also can be used to identify confusing or tedious elements of the program.

The following steps are taken:

Organizations can (optionally) first identify the cost of a dropout. This gives us a budget.

We then identify the behavior of dropouts. We study the data to look for patterns in the two minutes and seven minutes before dropping out.

Some questions considered:

- Is there a single place in the entire program where a disproportionate number of learners leave?
- Is there a single module?
- Is there a consistent type of engagement (linear, linear sim, linear activity, abstract sim, knowledge check, assessment)?
- Is there a consistent type of user behavior (such as multiple wrong answers) that leads to dropping out?

We then identify the opportunities for course improvement that either have a high ROI or very low cost. These may include changes to specific sections or a sweeping change over the whole program (such as every transition from sim back to linear).

As with performance, we can add *conviction* metrics to be used as statistical
50% proxies for dropouts where a correlation exists with actual dropouts. And as
with measuring performance, demographic data correlations with dropouts may
require different adjustments.

Other Uses of Tracking beyond Traditional Assessment

TADA (Teaching and Data Acquisition)

Teaching and Data Acquisition—a phrase coined by scholar Peter Shea—is an
emerging approach whereby educational content is used in an enterprise not
just to roll out best practices but to gain deeper insight into the environment.
Learning is two-way.

For example, consider a question in a refresher Short Sim for experienced
wholesale paint sellers. "You are selling paint to a potential customer who fixes
up rental condominiums. Do you emphasize a) Price per gallon, b) Price per coverage c) Durability, or d) Trendy colors?" While the rest of the Short Sim covers
new products and processes, the point of this interaction was to help corporate
understand what the field thought was important as input to marketing material.

These TADA questions can fit organically into a scenario, or they can be asked
explicitly. A coach may ask the player such questions as:

- You just closed a sale. Great! In your real job, what is the average length
  of time from getting a lead to closing a sale? [Less than one week, one to
  four weeks, More than four weeks.]

- Or "Well done on completing that situation. In your real job, in a week, how many times do you see your fellow health care workers do not wash their hands when they should?"

Players of Short Sim could be asked such questions as:

- What is a more valuable bonus: time off, a more interesting assignment, or a one-time lump of cash?
- Do they speak Chinese?
- What is the most important buying reason for cloud services over installed software?

In an environment of regular Short Sims deployment, most questions can be answered in twenty four hours.

Culture Dashboard

Using just the data from Short Sims currently gathered in the steps above, some organizations produce "heat maps" to visualize correlations between demographic categories (such as geography and role) and:

- Right and wrong answers;
- Start date and completion date, time on task;
- Readiness against certain key objectives.

These maps and other charts give organizations insight into which of their communities are healthier than others. Grey areas can identify specific skill and habit deficiencies or broader leadership concerns.

Uncovering Biases

Bias detection in a community can also be done in a Short Sim deployment.

For example, in part of a customer service course, an organization created situations where customers acted slightly suspiciously, and the learner had a choice as to whether to flag them or not. They made multiple versions of a sim, using the exact same situation with the same dialogue, but used avatars from two different nationalities or two different genders. By randomly using both versions and doing A/B testing, they gained insight into where biases existed.

Retries as a Surrogate Metric for Fun

Finally, while not strategic, I do want to mention one more trackable metric because it is the one I use more than the others. For more interesting sims, I like to measure engagement/fun. Specifically, I like to measure how often a player replays a Short Sim after they get a right answer. My ideal player-use pattern for a conviction building sim is:

- A player fails in the first two play throughs, then
- Discovers the right answer on the third, and then
- Plays through the sim two more times just to experiment in the world.

And More

There is so much more opportunity with tracking, from the clinical "A/B testing" to the more tricky gaining insight into a player's leadership style or ethics.

We are just beginning to peer into the power of tracking as an indispensable tool for instructional design. As we use more cloud-based services and have access to better visual presentation tools, this will give all of us the next level of power and speed, whatever the form of the content is.

Organization that Care about Metrics Will Prefer Short Sims

Most organizations in the education industry live and die by learner metrics. And those that use Short Sims get better metrics than those that use traditional content alone or full games.

- Traditional online learning today is linear. The "transcript" for each learner consists only of starts and stops, and perhaps how they did on some multiple choice questions.
- Perhaps worse, when used, computer game-like learning experiences produce too much data. Even after massive analysis, conclusions about learner behaviors are ambiguous.

Short Sims, however, produce streamlined transcripts of learners that can easily be acted upon. For most organizations, this will be the most compelling reason to adopt Short Sims.

22

Case Study
Creating a Simple Business Simulator

Short Sims can, in just a few minutes, allow players to gain a new perspective. This is a brief description of some design considerations for creating just such a Short Sim, to be used in a corporate environment for high potential, self-motivated employees. It rewards exploration and allows players to come to their own conclusions.

Unlike simpler examples, this sim shows a higher level of responsive design, potentially disqualifying it from the strictest definition of Short Sim.

Introduction

A leading credit card company wanted to develop in their employees a shared and deep understanding of payment systems, including the current mechanics and future opportunities. I was asked to build some Short Sims to support this program.

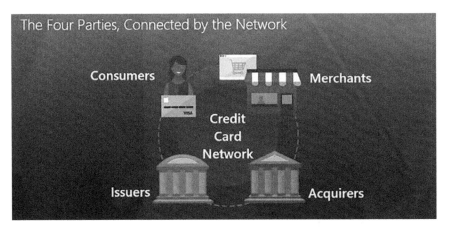

The Four Party Model

One of my sims had to help employees to think about merchants and the choices that merchants must make around payment systems, including the risks and opportunities.

A Growing Restaurant Chain, with a Technology Tree

After researching the topic, I decided to put the players in the position of a running and growing a smallish business, so the player would have a lot of control. Rather than retail, I chose a restaurant with three locations. That further allowed for interesting growth and evolution. The goal of the sim also had to match up with the real world—growing the business, impacted by the Four Party Model shown in the graphic above.

The next big design question was the interface. I wondered, would it be possible to have decisions around payment systems be the primary interface? Could a decision around, say, adopting Apple Pay change the direction of the company?

Then, I had to figure out the specific mechanisms. What would the player actually do, and how? One traditional type of B-school spreadsheet-based simulation asks players to make various allocation decisions around categories. "You have a lemonade stand and fifty dollars. How much do you want to spend on advertising versus ingredients versus staff for week 1?"

This seemed a bit too nebulous for a self-paced experience. What would be more interesting would be to have players, instead, make one big decision each turn for five turns. That could be more dramatic and more aligned with the Short Sims design principles, including *replayability*.

I thought through various business models and identified six enablers in which a restaurant entrepreneur may want to invest:

- Number of locations
- Payment options

- Big data and other tools of analysis
- Ability to do virtual or remote business
- Variety of things sold
- Branding.

Each turn, the player could invest in any one of these. After three turns, for example, the player could have added one point to the *Number of locations* enabler and two points to the *Branding* enabler.

Then, for each level per enabler, I added labels. For payment options, level zero was *cash and checks*, level one was *credit cards*, level two was *mobile systems*, and level three was *personalized coupons and special offers*. These labels were presented in the interface.

Finally, I added some interdependence. For example, the player had to begin taking credit cards before they launched a website. The mechanism allowed for an interesting and not quite easily predictable set of options each turn. It also allowed players to "discover" interesting options.

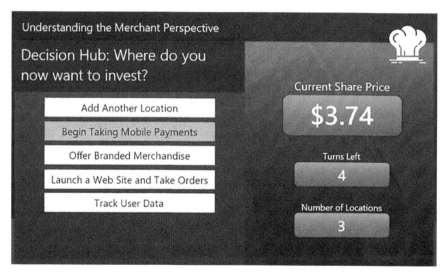

Options changed each turn

Some simple math associated with each level of each attribute would drive the share price.

Attribute Level Names

Achieving each new level of an attribute would present a graphic with a bit of description.

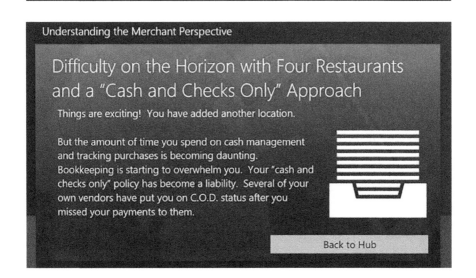

If players opened up too many stores without enabling credit cards, they ran into trouble.

The website option only opened up when a player began accepting credit cards.

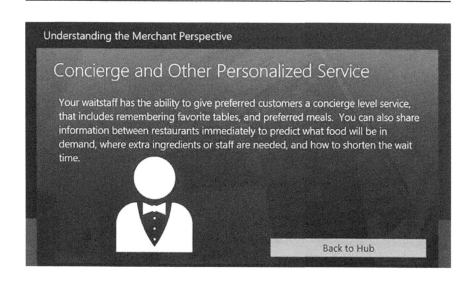

Some levels required several different prerequisites, including, in this case, credit cards and data collection.

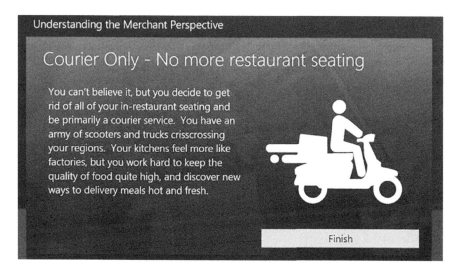

Achieving some enabler levels were dramatic, which would hopefully encourage replay and even comparisons with colleagues.

There were also a few additional pedagogical steps to reinforce key learning points.

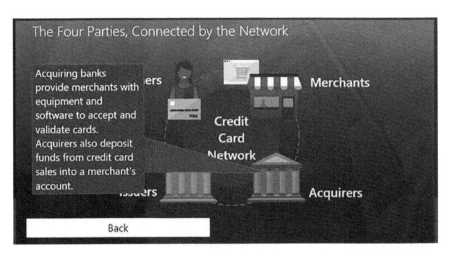

An interactive diagram presented the model

The end of game conclusion screens present a score in two forms, an open-ended share price and a star rating for easy comparison. Of course, in some cases, the restaurant went out of business. I also hoped that the players would be as interested in achieving the highest enabler levels than the score.

To see the sim:

- Spend five minutes and play it for yourself: www.shortsims.com/ch22
- Follow the walk-through in Appendix 7.

Conclusion

The payments learning program, of which this sim was part, was incredibly successful, with long waiting lists to participate and business transforming graduates.

This example turned out to be more extensive than a traditional Short Sim from a design perspective, but it did meet the needed criteria at both the client and player perspective. It aimed at a self-motivated audience, rewards exploration and replayability, and very quickly generated a new mindset and perspective. It allowed significant business model variation in a very short time and with very finite decisions. Any conversation about the sim could include, "what ending did you get and how did you get it," as much as "what was your score?" Most importantly, it positioned credit cards and the surrounding ecosystem in the situation of a growing business. Employees thinking about how to improve offerings would find their thinking and interest sharper in just a few minutes.

23

Conclusion

The biggest deal about Short Sims is that they don't feel like big deals.

Engaging a well-constructed example does not dazzle any user. It feels comfortable and familiar. This is because learning through interactivity is how our brains and bodies are designed to work.

It is only over time that we realize Short Sims are deconstructing the coping mechanisms built up from centuries of reliance on linear media. Shifting to a core of interactivity from a core of presentation opens up almost infinite possibilities.

Just a few:

- Short Sims can tackle tough topics where linear approaches have failed. They can help students become competent in ways that lectures, text, graphics, or videos simply can't. For schools to take on higher level and "learning to do" skills such as project management, stewardship, and leadership, new content is needed. Before Short Sims, that path didn't exist.
- Short Sims can develop conviction as well as competence. Overcoming all of Alan Kay's "universals"[1]—shifting from *superstition* to *science*, or *vendetta* to *laws* for example—requires building conviction.

- All big strategies in education—such as personalized and scalable learning, adaptive AI platforms, and more effective assessment—hinge on the effectiveness of the smallest pieces of content.
- A crisis in education today is the number of kinesthetic males for whom schools basically speak a foreign language. Short Sims can help bridge that gap. With Short Sims in schools, kinesthetic males can play the game first, not read the instruction manual first. They can invent their own theories, not study other people's. They can embrace the learning opportunity of mistakes, not try to avoid them at all costs. They can act like growing adolescents, not middle-aged adults.
- Short Sims also scale a more student-focused culture. Authors have to think about different students and different choices they may make. The leadership style that Short Sims should represent is collaborative, not directive.
- Corporations can now produce learning content at a high rate. One designer can create one Short Sim about every five to seven business days. If a company dedicated six designers, they could produce one short sim a day, creating an expectation of continuous shared learning. Any organization could burn through the list of outstanding requirements fairly quickly and get ahead of the backlog. In some cases, centralized modules could be customized by business divisions. And these learning modules could be two-way, providing key insights on all employees on different issues every day.
- And for those who believe that computer games are the manifest destiny of educational media, Short Sims get us there as well. By positing a thousand interfaces, and allowing the successful ones to evolve, we are laying a stronger foundation than any few game-based models ever could. (AI-augmented coding will be a necessary enabler of truly game-like educational experiences.)

For all of these reasons, and more, humble Short Sims may finally end education's dark ages and end up being a surprisingly big deal after all.

Appendix 1
Text Style Guide

Grammar and Punctuation Examples

Many Short Sims use words to do a lot of the heavy lifting. But it takes some back-end thought to make a text-based interface simple, intuitive, and nuanced. One key is the punctuation and syntax.

This example, called *Audio File*, employs a variety of text-based techniques:

- Use this link to Audio File: www.shortsims.com/ap01. Both the player and the onscreen coach are playing two roles, and the player's decisions include strategic intent as well as verbatim statements.

When One Type of Communication Is Used

In a traditional branching stories, the player may do nothing but talk to a single on screen avatar. In traditional game-based sims, the player may do nothing but issue commands. These can make due with sentences in the first situation and commands in the second.

Where the only user actions are commands to the sim, directive, title-case words are often best.

Options in Multi-Layer Sims

In other Short Sims, there may be more variety of communication. Three are most common:

1. The player may talk to the coach (i.e., What is my goal in this scenario?).
2. The player may issue commands, either to issue actions in a sim or to give high-level navigation orders ([Search for fingerprints on the glass.] or [Restart scenario.]).
3. The player may talk to characters in a role-play ("Perhaps you had better put the gun down.").

And text options may cover many of these, sometimes in the same line. It must be the role of a consistent syntax to make those options clear and seemingly invisible.

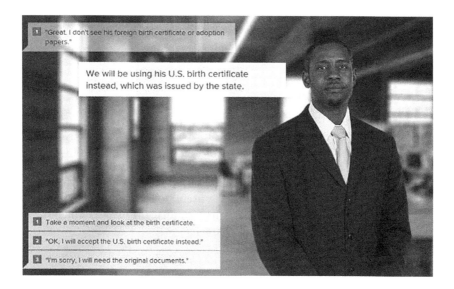

In this foreign adoption scenario, the player's options must differentiate between an *action* to perform (option 1, with no quotes) and *statements* to make (options 2 and 3, with quotes).

Here is one consistent punctuation style for a sim interface, when multiple modalities are used.

1. Sentence when the player communicates with the coach

    When a player interacts collaboratively with the coach, the statements have punctuation and first word capitalized. These are more conversational in tone.

    -   OK.
    -   What do you mean by that?
    -   Ready.
    -   Remind me about the policy.
    -   Great.
    -   Darn it all.
    -   Let's lower the price for now and see what happens.
    -   I've got an idea. [Lower the price.]
    -   Can you define the term more specifically?
    -   Fair enough.
    -   Thank you.

2. Meta-command to sim

    When the player is making a navigation or tactical-level command in a sim, or choosing an intent of a response in a role-play rather than the exact words, use brackets, title case, and punctuation. Imperative mood fragments are generally used.

- [Lower the price.]
- [Buy cats.]
- [Go back.]
- Never mind. [Go back.]
- [Show me the background again.]
- Forget it. [Take me back to the first choice.]

There can be *significant overlap* between the categories of talking to the coach and issuing commands to the sim, and there is often no right or wrong answer between brackets or not. It is at the discretion of the author in these cases. However, it is useful to err on the side of brackets when there is a chance the player may confuse the meta-command with a direct quote to the on screen character.

This sim does not use any coach, so quotations are not used. These statements combine actions and statements.

3. Player dialogue options in a role-play

When there is a coach present, but the player is talking to either an onscreen character (not the coach) or the coach playing the role of a character, use quotes.

- "I am doing fine, thank you."
- "Fine."
- First tell my partner, "Great," then make a sandwich.

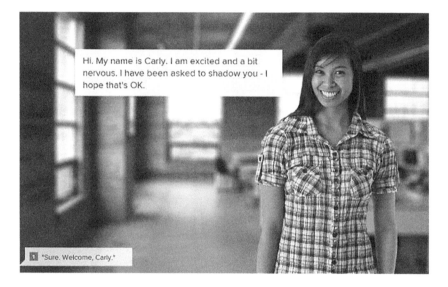

In a role-play with a coach, the character speaks without quotes, but the player speaks with them.

Coach Options

Most of the time, the coach (seen or not) speaks directly and without quotations.

Sometimes, as in the *Audio File* example above, the coach may take on the role of a role-playing character; in that situation, the coach in character speaks in quotes.

Other times, the coach may also speak for the player's character in a role-play. For example, where they player has a long answer, sometimes the Short Sim may present the beginning of the statement in quotes followed by an ellipse.

Where a long answer is advisable, the player may start the answer, but it will be finished by the coach in the next slide.

Then, the coach finishes your statement.

Role-Playing Character Options

The role-playing character does not use quotes unless a stage direction is also included, or the role-playing character is talking but we cut away, perhaps to a close up of a prop.

 OK. [Go back.]

"Yes. Here's my passport application."

1. [Take a few documents to look up on the Foreign Clearance Guide.] "I have to make sure a passport is needed for this assignment. This computer is not working right now, so I need to look this up at my desk."

2. [Take every document from the applicant to begin processing the application.] "Good, thanks. Let's make sure the right documents are here."

We use quotes around the role-play character's statement when we do not show them.

Specific Phrases

Some words or phrases have specific meanings, and should be used consistently across Short Sims.

- [Go back.]—Back up one decision, rewind.
- [Begin.]—Start the role-play section.
- OK.—Acknowledge and advance to the next slide. When there is a long text to be broken up, and presumably any acknowledgment on the part of the user would be premature, use instead [Next.]
- [Start over.]—Replay either the role-play portion or the entire Short Sim.
- [Try again.]—Replay the current level.
- [Skip to end.]—Skip to the last screen.
- [End sim.]—Use this to allow the user to end the entire experience. This is often used in conjunction with the option [Start over.]

While Editing

There may be some need to put in notes while creating a Short Sims, such as when art will be needed but not yet used. For there, I use double parentheses, such as ((Incomplete Form)).

Consistent Hierarchy/Generic Placement

Most Short Sims have between one and four commands available to a student. Whatever subsection of the list below is used, consider keeping the order consistent.

Hierarchy of Optional Options

- [Go back.]
- Ask for clarification of current state or goals
- Ask for other background information
- Choice 1/ Move forward./ Begin.
- Choice 2..N
- [Present other choices.]
- Re-present or provide more information about current options ("What are my choices right now," "Why can't I climb the tree?")
- [Skip ahead a little.]
- [Jump ahead a lot or back to Menu.]
- Detail the graphics or chart for disabled user
- [Restart.]
- [End sim.]

With careful writing, the options near the top represent more (optional) exploration. For example, two presented options may be

1. Before throwing out the trash, count the bottles.
2. Throw out the trash.

Here, the first step is an optional activity, before the fairly inevitable second activity. Depending on the situation, it may be a good choice if the user is being a detective, or a bad choice if the user is in a hurry or doesn't want to get caught.

Appendix 2

Examples of Learning Goals and Program Goals

With any program, one may identify specifically learning goals and program goals. Examples include

Learning Goals

- Is this target material for "learning to know," "learning to do," or "learning to be?"
- Is this about developing competence or conviction? Is this perpetuation or reinvention?
- Is this about doing the right thing or not doing the wrong thing? Is this learning something new or breaking old, bad habits?
- What is the "aha?" What is it that someone who knows this target material sees and does that is different than someone who does not? What is someone who knows this material tracking in a situation that is different than a naïve person?
- Produce some first person, specific examples of smart, dedicated people behaving differently for having learned this material compared to those who had not? Map it out step by step. Then, in examples of people

applying the naïve (pre-learning) behavior, what does failure look like to them? Is there one failure situation that you're trying to avoid, or a host of failures? What do experts do that is different?

- What are problems if this target material is not learned? If we don't do this, will there be visible (and measurable) negative consequences? What are they? Are these problems that will negatively impact the individual or the organization?
- Will we know if we are successful at an organization and individual level in developing these learning objectives in the target audience? How?
- Do we have identified experts, internally or externally, who do this well? Do we have genuine "best practices"?
- What part of this material is "Secret," compared to what part is organization specific (but not necessarily secret), and what part is "out there"?
- Is this something that has to be practiced?
- Is this content practicable in the real world? Will this content be practicable in the learning experience?
- Is this target material high-frequency use (something people use every day) or low (something that people might use in an emergency)?
- Will people know when they should be using this material? (Such as a client negotiation?)
- Is this something to learn just in case, just in time, or just for fun?
- Are there cultural advantages to many people adopting this content simultaneously?
- Do people already think they know this?
- What is the volume of people who will engage this program (number of students per year x number of years).
- What parts of this target material will change over time, and what parts will stay the same?
- Will this target material be consistent from participant to participant, or will it change? Will it change by language? By job role?
- Is this material being delivered and reinforced through other channels?
- Will someone be rewarded, intrinsically or extrinsically, for using this content in the productive world?
- Does this help the person do their day-to-day activities, or does it hinder them? (For example, information assurance programs can hinder day-to-day work.)
- Which groups in the organization most want the success of this material?
- Has this material been formally taught before? How, and to what success?
- Why this content now? What is the difference?
- How could mastery of this material be tested? Inside the program? Outside the program? What might happen if material is taken but not mastered by an individual?
- Is this the sole source of this material for the participants?

- *Real experts will also ask the following question*: are there bad or previously unintended consequences of people successfully learning this material?

Program Goals

- *Engagement*: Sims have to be engaging to students. To many people, that is their "reason for being." I would not argue that they have to be fun, but they do have to be fun enough. More than fun, they have to be immersive. Students can't be looking at the clock.
- *Convenient*: The work around accessing a sim has to be less than 5% of the total participation time for a student. They increasingly have to be accessed completely online. And they have to be short—about an hour for corporate employees, although easily ten or fifteen hours for academic environments. And they have to be well chunked.
- *Acceptable cost per student*: The cost per student has to be reasonable for the learning objectives, typically around $100 per corporate student and $45 per academic student.
- *Acceptable time to creation and delivery*: The time from approval to deliverable has to be around four months for a corporate environment, although up to one year for other environments.

Comfort level of implementers and sponsors: Finally, and most amorphously, the sponsors and implementers have to be comfortable with the material. They have to support it, understand it, and push for it. They have to believe in the material so completely that they will not accept failure.

Appendix 3

Broad List of Possible Subject Matter Expert Questions

Questions for Subject Matter Experts

For most sims, there are just two central questions for subject matter experts:

- What are the right ways of doing this?
- What are common mistakes in this area?

Then, organic expansions of this core question can sufficiently result in great Short Sims. Follow up questions include

- What happens when wrong decisions are made?
- Why do people make mistakes?
- What are tricky situations that may confuse newbies or experienced practitioners? Which situations would result in participants asking questions of colleagues, and which are mistakes people make without realizing they are making mistakes?
- What are different outcomes in this area, good and bad?

For *academics* or *consultants*, the questions are abstract and can alternatively include some subsection of

- What are situations that epitomized the subject matter? These can be microcosms, abstractions, and/or metaphors.
- In that situation, at multiple time intervals, what were the available options for someone involved? Was there a single "moment of truth?"
- At each of these moments, what might a naïve or inexperienced person do? What would an expert do?
- What does an expert know that an inexperienced person does not? (What "invisible" systems exist? Can relevant "invisible" systems be visualized? By metrics? Or maps? Are they dynamic and subtle or discrete?)
- What does success look and feel like? What does failure look and feel like? What are the short-term and long-term consequences? (Failure may look initially like success.)

Note: The challenge with content that has been processed through an academic lens is that it has been structured for linear content forms, including diagrams and case studies. A sim designer often has to scrape away these distractions and re-ask, always, "Who is doing the doing?"

Generic, probing questions for *authentic experts* who lived through the content can include

- What situation that you experienced epitomized the subject matter? (This could be a real-time meeting, or an event that took place over weeks, months, or years.) Were there multiple situations?
- What were your available options? At each moment, what could you have done in that situation, and what might a naïve or inexperienced person done? What did you end up doing?
- Why would the naïve approach fail? What would it not have taken into account?
- What were clues that you saw that informed your knowledge of the situation? What did you see immediately, and what information for which you had to look? How did you look for that information?
- What did you want success to be? What did the conclusion end up being?
- What were you looking for to suggest that things were going well? What were you looking for to suggest that things were not going well?
- What were the "maintenance" or routine activities that you had to do (even including body language) in the situation? What would happen if you did not do them?
- What was the moment were you knew you were successful? (Or not.)

These final questions are tougher, and therefore require a good relationships or otherwise goodwill with the subject matter expert:

- For the people involved, what was each's best-case and worst-case outcome? What were their strategies and actions?
- What would have been three to five legitimate alternative approaches to the problem or situation?
- What were the three to five high-level issues that you were monitoring? Time? Commitment? Alignment? What trade-offs were you willing to make? What trade-offs did you make? Can you graph the high-level metrics over the course of the experience? What were the inflection points for each? How do the actions impact the high-level metrics? What else impacts the high-level metrics?

Terms Used in Initial Processing of Subject Matter Expert Interviews

Notes should be taken from interviews that fall into the following categories:

Category	Description	Econ 101: International Trade Example (Chapter 15)	Linear Process Example: DOD Passport Acceptance Agent
Starting points, types of challenges, unusual circumstances	The condition that begins the sim, which can include an erroneous mindset.	Students think of international trade in terms of a zero-sum negotiation.	A soldier applies for a passport because she will be deployed abroad.
Successful outcomes	What success looks like. This could be for the entire experience, or just at one point in the process.	Students understand how to determine which country should be producing a product based on the concept of relative advantage.	Passport agents looks up in online tool that the destination, say Germany or Japan, does not need a passport, so does accept application.
Unsuccessful outcomes	What failure looks like.	Students make decisions based on absolute advantage.	Passport agency submits a passport application for an unnecessary passport, or hands back to soldier application after it has been accepted.

(Continued)

Category	Description	Econ 101: International Trade Example (Chapter 15)	Linear Process Example: DOD Passport Acceptance Agent
Moments of truth and interesting decisions, problems, fixes, best practices	What are decisions that can make a situation better or worse, or lead to absolute success or failure	Students choose which country has a production advantage.	Whether or not to accept a passport application.
Milestones and influences— story beats, rules, or correct sequences.	Situations between the beginning and end that change or evolve the direction of the story or are a necessary step in the process. (These can be included as midpoints in longer sims or may instead turned into starting points for short levels.)	Students think in terms of opportunity costs.	Verifying travel orders; the commanding officer wants the soldier to have a passport just-in-case she needs it for subsequent deployments.
Interesting facts and phrases, background notes	Facts that are either important or interesting, that should work their way into either set ups, conclusions, or somewhere else.	According to Econ 101 theory, when both sides engage in trade, both sides come out better off;	DOD passport agencies can only issue special passports in the States, but can also issue "tourist" passports overseas.

Appendix 4
Be a Hacker Walk-Through

While playing the sim is the best way to go experience the content, this walk-through is a typical engagement.

The setup is simple:

We are quickly given the core choice, but also likely suspect some kind of trickery:

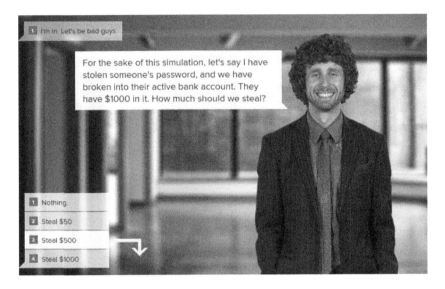

One safe-feeling option is to take a lot of money, but not all of it:

The coach pushes us

We are back at the beginning, but with a bit of experience under our belts, so we see things a bit differently:

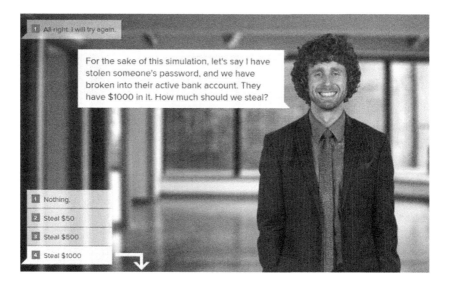

We are a bit more emboldened:

We then face a new, big idea:

The sim is voluntary. We have the choice to end it, and we are always given a way out, just as we are coaxed to continue:

A big idea and challenge is reintroduced:

Now we try one of the few options left:

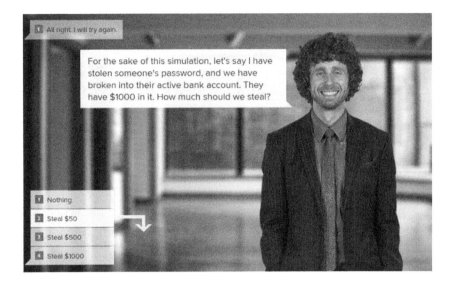

There is a new option that intrigues us a bit:

Now, we smile and start to see the answer:

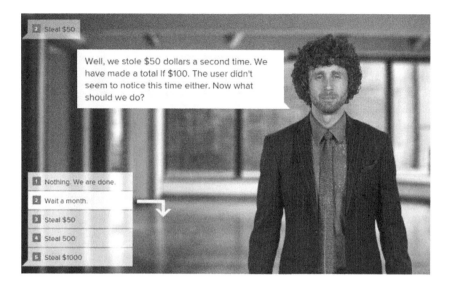

The sim now anticipates our budding awareness and stays just slightly ahead of us:

The sim plays out what happens next and also lets us know this is the best outcome for this experience:

The big "aha" of the sim is presented explicitly to us.

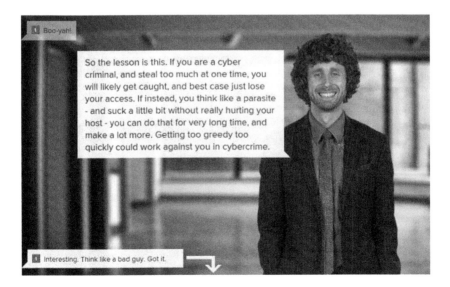

The ending is satisfying, as a bit of a surprise but not in some cheap trick way. It does not feel as if we were set up. The conclusion feels real.

As might a waiter at the end of the meal, the coach appreciates our time and interest:

Appendix 5
Short Walk-Through of Visual Problem Identification

Visual decision-making is another technique to obscure the right answer in a multiple choice interface. This minilab first asks the player if there is a problem, as it already has several previous steps so far.

1 OK

You see the place of birth.

1 [Accept and move on]
2 [Ask a question]

It again allows the player to accept the situation and move on, or dig in. (The black triangles are used to indicate the option selected.)

 [Ask a question.]

> You ask the applicant for his birthplace, and
> the applicant says quickly and comfortably,
> "Columbia, Missouri."

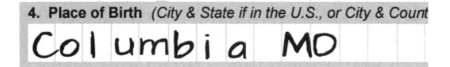

1 [Accept and move on.]

2 Don't move on yet. I see a problem. ◀

Once the player has acknowledged there is a problem, the player then has to identify it. Here, the player cycles through three possibilities of problems, with the consistent fourth option being to move on and accept the form.

Possibility one of three:

2 Don't move on yet. I see a problem.

Is "Columbia" the problem?

1 No. It is something else. ◀

2 Yes. This is the problem.

3 Never mind. The birthplace part of the application seems fine to me.

Possibility two of three:

1 No. It is something else.

Is this part the problem?

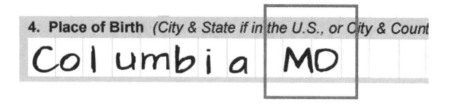

1 No. It is something else. ◀

2 Yes. This is where the problem is.

3 No. Never mind. This part of the application seems fine

Possibility three of three:

1 No. It is something else.

Is the whole thing the problem?

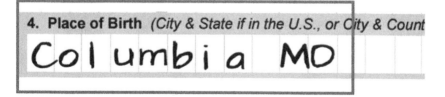

1 No. It is something else. ◀

2 Yes. This is where the problem is.

3 Never mind. The birthplace part of the application seems fine to me.

After the optional process of cycling through and considering everything (and one could easily write the sim such that the player only has one chance to find the problem, which may better evaluate conviction levels), the player does find the problem.

1 OK. Where else might there be a problem?

Is this part the problem?

4. Place of Birth *(City & State if in the U.S., or City & Count*

Col umbi a MO

1 No. It is something else.

2 Yes. This is where the problem is. ◀

3 No. Never mind. This part of the application seems fine.

This leads to the coach presenting a wrap up of the learning objective.

If, as happened in this sim, at most steps the player is asked if something is wrong, and further identification is required if the answer is "yes," then players become gun shy to claim something is wrong unless they actually see something. It reduces fishing expeditions. It is also an example of how a consistent interface—always asking if there is a problem—can hide the right answer in plane site by desensitizing the player to an option that will eventually be critical, a technique necessary for most interesting sims.

Appendix 6

Simple Business Simulator Walk-Through

The client wanted to give their students a deeper understanding of the credit card ecosystem. In this sim, the students play one part, the merchants, and make a series of business-changing decisions that emphasize how important payment systems are.

- Engage it here: www.shortsims.com/ap07

Walk-through:

1. The sim sets up the situation.

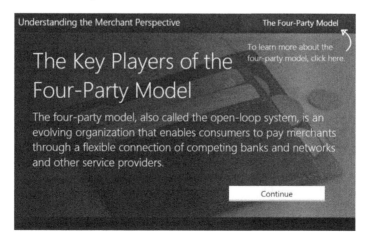

2. The starting narrative is pretty simple, as is the score card of "share price."

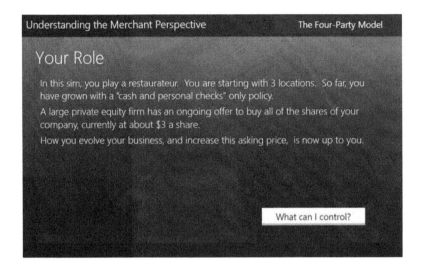

3. The sim will limit the player to a small number of turns, with each turn allowing just one decision to improve one enabler. All enablers are organized into six categories.

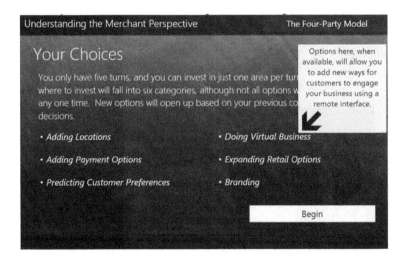

4. This sim uses mouse-overs throughout to learn more about options. More open-ended interfaces such as this one should always use some kind of animation to let players know where they hot spots are.

5. Now we begin the sim. In the first turn, we see just three enablers on the left, in the three enabler categories of adding locations, adding payment options, and expanding retail options. The relevant dashboard information is on the right. The player chooses to spend their turn to adopt credit cards.

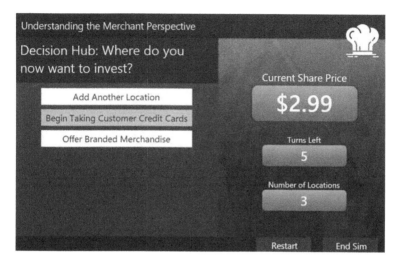

6. Every decision, including this decision to adopt credit cards, is costly; it uses up the turn. In this case, the sim presents a follow-up strategic choice that is consistent with the choice that many vendors make around accepting credit cards: legacy or leading edge. This choice does impact the availability of advancement opportunities in certain categories of business enablers. For example, if a player chooses legacy terminals, they cannot later upgrade to accept mobile payments.

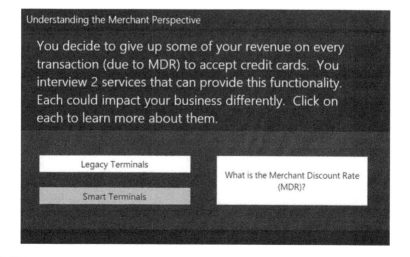

7. A bit of content is presented. For the target audience (employees of a credit card company), this is not a bad time to learn a bit about some of the features. They player here chooses smart terminals.

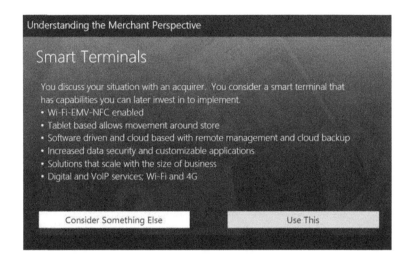

8. With the adoption of credit cards and smart terminals, more options are now opened up. The payment button has been replaced with a mobile payments options, and a few new options have been unlocked.

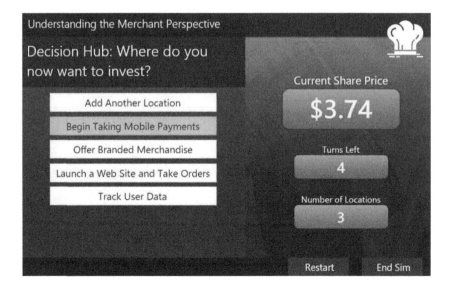

9. Each time a player improves an attribute, he or she gets a screen to confirm and explain.

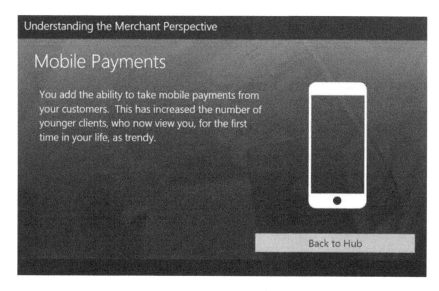

10. We see a tick up in our score and a tick down in the number of turns left. While there are currently no payments options (others will only appear based on subsequent decisions), we still have four decisions. We decide to track user data.

11. The feedback here is that this option does not have an immediate payoff, but is just an enabler.

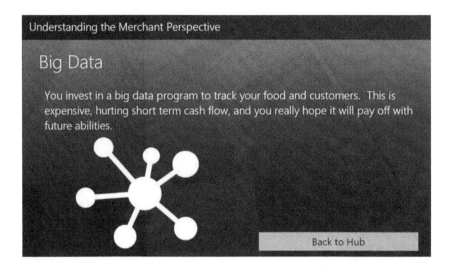

12. We can see that due to the expense, our share price went down, but we have earned more options. The payment section now has "custom coupons," for example. Here, I added a bit of a cheat, which is an option for the player to earn an extra turn by answering a question.

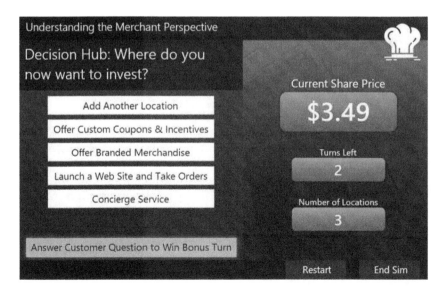

13. Here is the question, which aligns with the strategic goals of the program without breaking the mood too much:

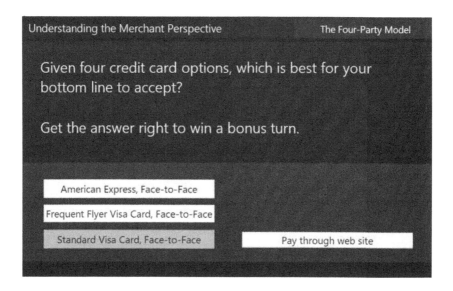

14. The player answers it correctly. Key terms are introduced organically.

15. The player has an extra turn—our primary currency—to use. We choose branded merchandise.

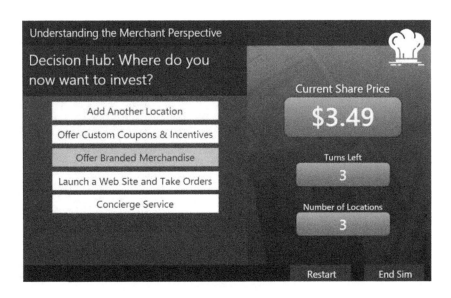

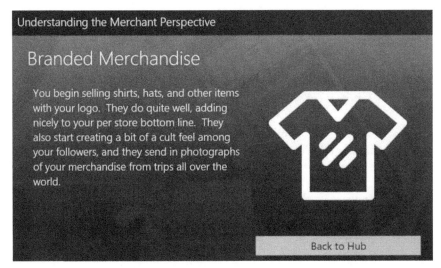

16. This opens up the next level of the enabler *Variety of things sold*, which is pre-packaged food. We do that next.

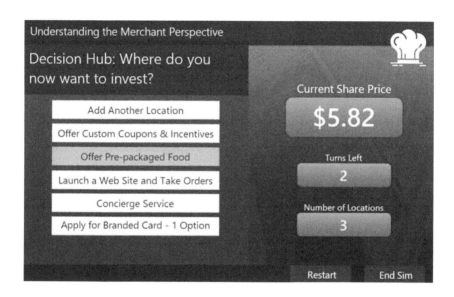

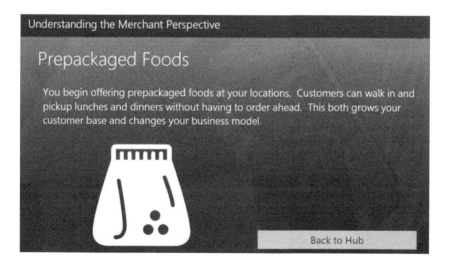

17. We now have one turn left. We go more extreme.

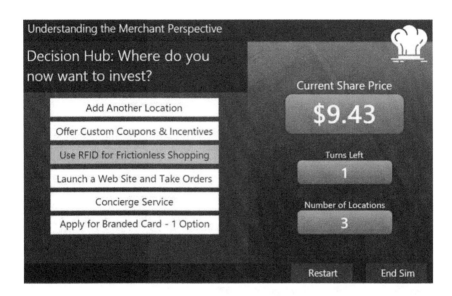

18. We are now at the end of our journey. Through specific decisions, we have arrived at an entirely new business model, enabled by payment systems.

19. The final screen shows a score (the share price), a star rating (so players can know how they did), and a bit of a summary. Many players will play a second or third time, making different decisions, and will be rewarded with significantly different businesses. The sim is a challenge, not to get the best score, but to rethink credit card services to enable business growth and reinvention.

Glossary

Here is a glossary of relevant terms.
    Many will refer to the core mechanic of a Short Sim.

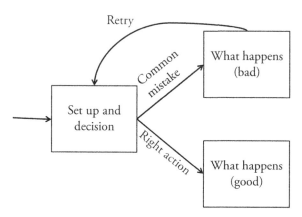

A Core Mechanic of Developmental Short Sims.

architecture: The combination of nodes and connections that contain how a Short Sim is put together. This may also be called a *chart*. See the figure below.

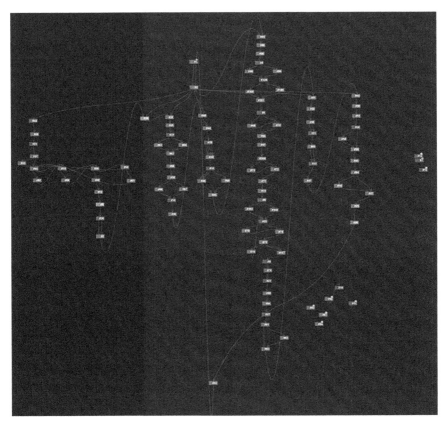

Almost done architecture

art: Visual elements for the interface. Art can include avatars, backgrounds, or charts, depictions, or elements superimposed on the background, such as a map. Art can be *off-the-shelf* or custom. (Aka *Art assets*.)

avatar: The representation of a character on screen, in the *interface*. This supports, but is not synonymous with, a personality or character in a sim. For example, a *sim* may have a consistent personality for a coach that is never visually shown, by using text boxes.

backdrop: The image (or video) that fills the screen, and is behind any avatar and player options. The backdrop can be a generic scene to place the events. If so, the picture is often a bit out of focus. This type of backdrop can be consistent throughout an entire *level* or *sim*. Alternatively, the backdrop can present some visual information that is critical to meet the pedagogical goals of the sim.

beats, story: Important moments that have to happen and that impact a narrative trajectory, either speeding it up, slowing it down, or changing it.

coach: A special character in a Short Sim that talks and works directly with the user. A coach may be similar in role to the acting coach in a scene workshop. They provide instructions and encouragement. They set up a role-play, and may interrupt it to ask questions or make a point. A coach can also present impacts, good or bad, of decisions.

cognitive load: The amount of new information a player has to hold in his or her head in order to proceed in a simulation. Every new character and situation, for example, increases the cognitive load. Confusing wording or interfaces can increase the cognitive load. The goal for most Short Sims, unless there is a specific pedagogical objective to be met, is to minimize the cognitive load for the player.

conviction: A strong belief in the importance of something. Many learning goals, such as getting learners to not text while driving, show all work, or trust science over superstition, require conviction building.

decision: Of the possible *options* on screen, the one that the player engages.

decision menu: The collection of player *options* presented, from which the player must choose one. Also called *Option menu*. In some cases, a sim may not have an established menu, such as if the action required is to click on some hot spots on an image or *slide*.

developmental short sim: A Short Sim that is designed to educate a user, rather than one that is designed to assess a user.

educational simulation: Abstracted *simulation* with additional framing content, designed to develop skills or understanding in a user (e.g., flight simulators).

first person: Tethering a perspective in media to a character in the world portrayed. In a first person Short Sim, the player takes the perspective of being in the world, and making decisions that impact that world. A first person perspective encourages a learning to do philosophy.

forked copy: A second version of a given sim that has certain key elements changed. Forking a sim means that two (or more) versions have to be updated independently when certain content changes or mistakes are found.

gamification: Using framing content designed to make any activity more like a game and/or addictive. Enduring games are created when one adds gamification techniques on top of simple, enjoyable tasks (throwing a ball in a hoop, controlling an on screen avatar to jump over a moving object), voluntarily engaged, by adding layers of strategy, feedback, competition, and complexity.

interface: The information presented to the user of sim, and the presentation (explicit or implicit) of actions a user can take. Some actions can be presented as multiple choice, and others may be other hot spots.

learning objective: Any identified competence or conviction that has been identified for a given learning program to develop.

narrative branch: Decisions that initiative two or more distinct stories, with different decisions and feedback. A branched narrative can selectively re-integrate. See the figure below.

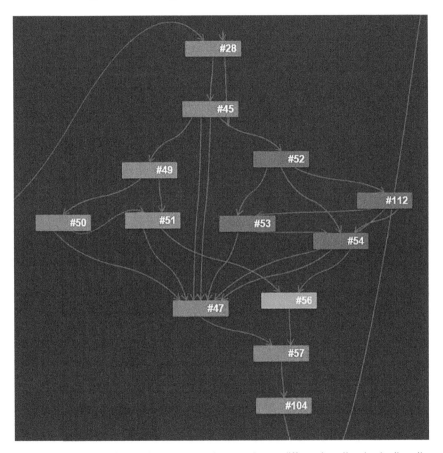

Here, choices made in #45 can take players down different paths, including the right and wrong paths. The narrative re-integrates at #57.

option: A choice that the player can make to progress in a simulation. Some represent decisions that are big, such as deciding to take a job, or flip a big switch that says, "do not touch." Some decisions are small, such as raising the price by ten cents or putting your left foot in. These will all be reflected in a node's interface. Oxymoronically, in many screens, there is only one choice presented.

player: The person who engages the short sim as a participant. Also called *student* (in a more academic context), *learner,* or *user.*

response: One common use for a *player option*. A *decision* includes more than one possible response.

retry: A moment in a Short Sim when the player, having made a mistake, goes back and is given the same opportunity to make another choice.

sequence: What may happen in a sim, from beginning to end. This could be how to make a cake, or how a story unfolds. The sequence is the "how" of content, while often the setup is the "why." All sims have at least one main sequence. Some sims have many different overlapping sequences. Some sequences will include failures as well as successes. A sequence can apply to a single level.

serious games: Educational material with additional framing content designed to make the learning fun and/or addictive, or games with educational elements (e.g., game shows or SimCity).

setup: Situations that designers create for the player to engage. What role is the player taking on, and what are the goals? Identifying a good setup for some sims is easy and obvious, for others, quite hard.

Short sim: A sim distilled to its educational essence in design and production; a sim of a sim.

sims: Interactive educational experiences that include both *educational simulations* and *serious games*.

simulation: Functioning model of something else, designed for accuracy and predictiveness.

slide: A predefined short sim state that includes through which players can traverse. Slides can include the consequence from the last decision; setup for the next decision; the presentation of player options (including responses); one or more avatars; and *backdrops*. Also called *Node* (used when the designer is looking "zoomed out" at the connections between states), *Screen* (which consists of all of the information the player sees, which could even include information around the sim, if the sim is embedded in document or LMS), *Scene* (when thinking about the characters and consequences), *Event, Panel, Frame, Cell,* and *Page. Slide* may be a default term when thinking about partitioning up content, and builds from one to the next.

small and medium size enterprise (SME): What everyone else thinks you mean when you refer to an *SME*.

SME: A subject matter expert, such as Karl Kapp on gamification.

starting point: The condition that begins the sim, which can include an erroneous mindset.

subject matter expert (SME): A person who knows a significant amount on the topic at hand. Research generally includes interviewing one or more subject matter experts.

successful outcome: An end to a *sim, level,* or other challenge that represents a positive, usually sought after outcome. This *can* include meeting the explicit goals presented at the beginning of the sim. Successful outcomes may be presented in narrative form, high scores, or "stars" (i.e., three out of four stars).

unsuccessful outcomes: An end to a sim, level, or other challenge that represents a negative, usually avoided outcome. These may terminate the sim, allow players to move on, or force them to retake the section they failed. Some negative outcomes are fun for the player to invoke and can also be educational.

Index

Theory of the case, 148–151; *see also* Invisible system
Time sucks, 22
Tolerance for ambiguity, 26, 133
Twine, 6
Two-Sided Markets sim, 160–163

U

Unforced decisions, 129
Unsuccessful outcome, *see* Failure
User actions, 2, 111, 118, 162, 196; *see also* Decision; Multiple choice

V

Victory condition, 117, 119, 121, 154; *see also* Goal, player
Virtual Leader, *see* SimuLearn's Virtual Leader
Visual element, 110; *see also* Lab; Mini-map
Visual problem solving (visual decision making, visual problem identification), 48–53, 223–226; *see also* Lab

Printed and bound by CPI Group (UK) Ltd, Croydon, CR0 4YY

01/11/2024

01782616-0011